PRIMER OF LABOR RELATIONS

A Guide to Employer-Employee Conduct

HOWARD J. ANDERSON

Senior Editor for Labor Services
The Bureau of National Affairs, Inc.

Twentieth Edition

Published 1975 by

THE BUREAU OF NATIONAL AFFAIRS, INC.

WASHINGTON, D.C.

International Standard Book Number: 0-87179-046-7
Library of Congress Catalog Number: 56-2617

Printed in the United States of America

CONTENTS

THE LAW OF LABOR RELATIONS:
A BIRD'S-EYE VIEW

The federal law governing labor relations rests on three basic statutes, the first adopted in 1935 and the other two at 12-year intervals thereafter. These laws—the Wagner, Taft-Hartley, and Landrum-Griffin Acts—provide the foundation for a complex structure of rules, regulations, and decisions.

THE WAGNER ACT

In adopting the Wagner Act or National Labor Relations Act in 1935, Congress established the principle that the employees should be protected in their rights to organize into labor organizations and to bargain collectively concerning their wages and working conditions. To provide this protection, the Act made it an unfair labor practice for an employer to do any of the following:

► Interfere with, restrain, or coerce employees in the exercise of their rights to organize, bargain collectively, and engage in other concerted activities for their mutual aid or protection.

► Dominate or interfere with the formation or administration of any labor organization or contribute financial or other support to it.

► Encourage or discourage membership in any labor organization by discrimination with regard to hiring or tenure or conditions of employment, subject to an exception for valid union-security agreements.

► Discharge or otherwise discriminate against an employee because he has filed charges or given testimony under the Act.

► Refuse to bargain collectively with the majority representative of his employees.

In addition to forbidding the five employer unfair labor practices, the Act set up election machinery to permit employees to choose collective bargaining representatives. The National Labor Relations Board was created to administer and enforce the Act.

1

THE TAFT-HARTLEY ACT

In the 12 years following the enactment of the Wagner Act, many members of Congress became convinced that the balance in labor-management relations had become too heavily weighted in favor of the unions. They believed that employers and employees needed protection against unfair practices of unions and that the public needed protection against labor disputes resulting in work stoppages that threatened the national health or safety.

The Taft-Hartley Act adopted in 1947 sought to provide such protection and restore the balance in labor relations. The new law was built upon the framework of the Wagner Act, retaining the provisions for exclusive representation of employees by majority bargaining agents and the restrictions on unfair labor practices of employers. But virtually all of the Wagner Act's major provisions were amended or qualified in some respect, and an entirely new code of conduct for unions and their agents was established.

In addition to the five employer unfair practices forbidden by the Wagner Act, the Taft-Hartley Act forbade a series of unfair labor practices by unions. It became unlawful for a union to do any of the following:

▶ Restrain or coerce employees in the exercise of their rights under the Act.

▶ Restrain or coerce an employer in the selection of his bargaining or grievance representative.

▶ Cause or attempt to cause an employer to discriminate against an employee on account of his membership or non-membership in a labor organization, subject to an exception for valid union-shop agreements.

▶ Refuse to bargain collectively (in good faith) with an employer if the union has been designated as bargaining agent by a majority of the employees.

▶ Induce or encourage employees to stop work for an object of forcing an employer or self-employed person to join a union or of forcing an employer or other person to stop doing business with any other person (secondary boycott).

▶ Induce or encourage employees to stop work for an object of forcing an employer to recognize and bargain with the union where another union has been certified as bargaining agent (strike against a certification).

▶ Induce or encourage employees to stop work for an object of forcing an employer to assign particular work to members of the union instead of to members of another union (jurisdictional strike).

▶ Charge an excessive or discriminatory fee as a condition to becoming a member of the union.

▶ Cause or attempt to cause an employer to pay for services that are not performed or not to be performed (featherbedding).

The Taft-Hartley Act also made some important changes in the rules for representation elections. The NLRB's discretion in determining appropriate units was limited, replaced economic strikers lost their voting rights, the Board was barred from conducting more than one election a year in a particular unit, and a number of other changes were made in the election machinery.

THE LANDRUM-GRIFFIN ACT

The adoption of the third basic federal labor law, the Labor-Management Reporting and Disclosure Act of 1959, was triggered by the disclosures of the McClellan Committee. In two and one-half years of investigation and public hearings, the Committee compiled an imposing record of wrongdoing on the part of certain unions and their officers, of coercion of employees and small employers, and of shady dealings and interference with employees' rights by "middlemen" serving as management consultants. The Act was aimed at eliminating these practices.

Essentially, the 1959 Act was two statutes. First, there was a code of conduct for unions, union officers, employers, and consultants. Second, there was a group of significant amendments to the Taft-Hartley Act, amendments that both modified existing provisions and added entirely new provisions.

The code of conduct guarantees certain inalienable rights to union members within their union and imposes certain obligations on unions, union officers, employers, and consultants. In brief, this is what the code does:

▶ Every labor organization is required to have a constitution and by-laws containing certain minimum standards and safeguards. Reports on the union's policies and procedures, as well as annual financial reports, must be filed with the Secretary of Labor and must be disclosed to the union's members.

▶ Union members have a bill of rights to protect their rights within the union.

▶ Standards are established for union trusteeships and union elections. Reports on trusteeships must be made to the Secretary of Labor.

▶ A fiduciary obligation is imposed on union officers, and they are required to file reports with the Secretary of Labor on conflict-of-interest transactions.

▶ Employers and labor relations consultants are required to file reports on expenditures and arrangements that affect employees' organizing and bargaining rights.

▶ The Secretary of Labor is made the watchdog of union conduct. He is the custodian of reports from unions and their officers, and he is given the power to investigate and prosecute violations of many of the provisions of the Act.

THE 1959 TAFT-HARTLEY AMENDMENTS

The amendments to the Taft-Hartley Act included in the 1959 Reform or Landrum-Griffin Act were a blend of so-called labor sweeteners, sought by the unions, and additional restrictions on the unions' strike, picketing, and boycott weapons, sought by the employers. But the additional restrictions appeared in some respects to have outweighed the labor sweeteners. In brief, here is what the amendments did:

▶ State courts and labor relations boards were given jurisdiction over cases rejected by the NLRB under its jurisdictional standards. This eliminated the "no-man's land" created by the Supreme Court's Guss decision.

▶ Permanently replaced economic strikers were given the right to vote in representation elections conducted by the NLRB within one year after the beginning of the strike, subject to regulations to be issued by the NLRB.

▶ Three loopholes in the secondary-boycott prohibition apparently were closed, and hot-cargo agreements were outlawed, subject to exceptions relating to subcontracting in the construction and garment industries.

▶ A new unfair labor practice made it unlawful for a union to picket for recognition or organizational purposes under certain circumstances.

▶ Pre-hire and seven-day union shop contracts were legalized in the construction industry.

The Taft-Hartley Act, as amended, appears at LRX 3751; the Landrum-Griffin Act is at LRX 7001.

HOSPITAL AMENDMENT

In 1974, Congress passed an amendment extending the coverage of the Act to private nonprofit hospitals and nursing homes. The NLRB already had asserted jurisdiction over proprietary hospitals and nursing homes by decision.

The amendment, however, does not extend to hospital employees a protected right to strike. But it provides for compulsory mediation of hospital disputes by the Federal Mediation and Conciliation Service.

OTHER FEDERAL LABOR LAWS

There are a number of other important federal labor laws. Some preceded the National Labor Relations Act; others followed it. They deal with a wide range of subjects—railway labor disputes, labor injunctions, minimum wages, strikebreakers, labor racketeering, and private pension plans. Following are capsule summaries of what these other laws do.

Railway Labor Act—Adopted in 1926 and amended in 1934, 1951, and 1966, this law provides a means of naming bargaining agents for employees of carriers through elections conducted by the National Mediation Board. It also provides some dispute-settlement and arbitration procedures. In brief, these procedures are as follows:

▶ Disputes over the interpretation or application of collective bargaining contracts in the railroad industry that are not resolved by the parties may be referred by either party to the National Railroad Adjustment Board. Although recourse to the Adjustment Board is voluntary, an award made by the Board is enforceable in court. The 1966 amendments also provided for limited judicial review of awards on suit by either party.

▶ A railroad or union desiring to make a change in wages, rules, or working conditions must give at least 30-days' written notice. If the proposed change results in a dispute, either party may request the services of the National Mediation Board or the Board may proffer its services if it finds that a labor emergency exists. If the Board fails to resolve the dispute by mediation, it then must try to induce the parties to submit the dispute to binding arbitration.

▶ When all of these procedures fail and a strike is threatened, the President is authorized to appoint an emergency board to investigate and report to the President concerning the dispute within 30 days after it is created. Until the emergency board reports and for 30 days thereafter, strikes and lockouts are forbidden, although no penalty is provided for violating the ban.

In 1936, all provisions of the Act except those relating to the Adjustment Board were made applicable to air carriers and their employees. Instead of a national adjustment board, each air carrier and the representatives of its employees must establish a system board of adjustment to resolve disputes as to the meaning and application of their contracts.

The Railway Labor Act appears at LRX 6001.

Norris-LaGuardia Act—Adopted in 1932 to prevent abuse of injunctions in labor disputes, the Norris-LaGuardia Anti-injunction Act (LRX 3501) forbids the federal courts to issue injunctions in labor disputes except under strictly limited conditions. Before an injunction may be issued, it must be shown, among other things, that there were prior efforts to settle the dispute peaceably, that law-enforcement officials are unable or unwilling to safeguard the employer's property, and that a denial of an injunction will entail greater loss to the employer than granting it will cause to the union. No injunctions may be issued aainst peaceful picketing. The Act also outlawed the "yellow dog" contract under which a worker, as a condition of employment, agrees not to join or remain a member of a union.

The Taft-Hartley and Landrum-Griffin Acts made some exceptions to the Norris-LaGuardia Act.

Antistrikebreaking Act—The Byrnes Antistrikebreaking Act of 1938 (LRX 4401) forbids the interstate transportation of persons to be used to interfere with peaceful picketing in a labor dispute or with the processes of collective bargaining.

Antiracketeering Acts—The Hobbs Antiracketeering Act of 1946 (LRX 7501) forbids criminal conspiracy to impede interstate commerce by extortion or robbery. As adopted in 1934, the Act exempted "the payment of wages by a bona fide employer to a bona fide employee." The Supreme Court in 1942 construed this exemption to protect a member of a truckers' union against prosecution for stopping trucks operated by nonunion employees and compelling them to pay sums of money equivalent to the union pay scale. (10 LRRM 368) The Act was amended by Congress in 1946 to delete the exemption. Violators are subject to criminal penalties.

The Lea Act of 1946 (LRX 7601) forbids coercion of broadcasting companies to agree to hire employees whose services are not needed.

Wage-Hour Laws—There are a number of federal laws setting wage-hour standards for employees engaged in interstate commerce or government-contract work. The Fair Labor Standards Act (LRX 8101) establishes minimum-wage, overtime, and child-labor standards for employees engaged in interstate commerce or the production of goods for interstate commerce. The Walsh-Healey Act (LRX 8301) establishes similar standards for employees working on government supply contracts. The Davis-Bacon, Contract Work Hours Standards, and Copeland Antikickback Acts (LRX 8001, 8051, 8071) establish minimum-wage, fringe-benefit, and overtime standards for employees working on government-financed construction projects. The Fair Labor Standards Act was amended in 1963 to forbid wage differentials based solely on sex, effective in June 1964. Coverage, minimum-wage and other changes were made by amendments in 1949, 1961, and 1966.

The Service Contracts Act of 1965 requires employers performing service contracts for government agencies to pay their employees not less than the minimum wages and fringe benefits found by the Secretary of Labor to be prevailing locally. In no event, may they pay their employees less than the minimum wage under the Fair Labor Standards Act.

Welfare Fund Disclosure—The Welfare and Pension Plans Disclosure Act (LRX 8551) adopted by Congress in 1958 requires administrators of employee welfare and pension plans to make detailed reports to participants and the Secretary of Labor. The reports must disclose the terms of the plans and their financial operations. In 1962, the Act was amended to give the Secretary of Labor interpretative, investigative, and enforcement powers. Kickbacks, embezzlement, conficts of interest, and false entries by fund officials or employees were made federal crimes subject to stiff penalties. The Employee Retirement Income Security Act, adopted in 1974, established additional fiduciary standards for plan administrators. It also provided for mandatory vesting of benefits and funding of plans. An agency was established in the Labor Department to insure benefits in the event of the termination of a plan.

Equal Employment Opportunity—Title VII of the Civil Rights Act of 1964 makes it unlawful for employers, labor unions, and employment agencies in industries affecting interstate commerce to discriminate in employment or union membership against any individual because of his race, color, religion, sex, or national origin. The provisions of Title VII are administered by an Equal Employment Opportunity Commission. Prior to April 24, 1972, the Commission was limited to seeking compliance through a system of formal and informal remedial procedures, including conference, conciliation, and persuasion. But it could not bring an action in court against an employer, union, or employment agency alleged to have violated the Act. Aggrieved employees, however, could sue upon a finding by the Commission of reasonable cause to believe a violation had been committed—a requirement construed liberally by the courts to permit aggrieved individuals to assert their rights where the Commission delayed in processing a charge. The Justice Department also was authorized to bring an action where it found an alleged "pattern or practice" of violation.

On April 24, 1972, President Nixon signed the Equal Employment Opportunity Act of 1972, authorizing the Commission to bring an action in a federal district court where it found reasonable cause to believe a violation had been committed. If the Commission failed to sue, the aggrieved individuals could bring an action themselves. Jurisdiction to bring "pattern or practice" actions was to be shared with the Department of Justice for two years; thereafter the Commission would have exclusive jurisdiction over such actions. In the first action brought under the amended Act, a federal district court in Florida held that the Commission must go through all the procedural steps specified in the Act, including efforts to resolve the case through conference, conciliation, and persuasion, before bringing an action in court. (5 FEP Cases 108)

The 1972 Act also extended the coverage of Title VII. The most important change was that which made state and local governments subject to the prohibitions. Enforcement of the Act in this area, however, was assigned to the Justice Department rather than to the Commission.

The text of Title VII, as amended, appears at LRX 1801.

In 1967, Congress enacted the Age Discrimination in Employment Act. Effective June 12, 1968, this Act made it unlawful for an employer, an employment agency, or a labor union to discriminate in employment against persons in the 40-to-65 age bracket. The task of administering and enforcing the Act was given to the Secretary of Labor, who delegated the job to the Wage and Hour and Public Contracts Divisions.

The text of the Age Discrimination in Employment Act appears at LRX 1815.

The NLRB also has moved into this area of discrimination under the Taft-Hartley Act. It has held that a labor union that discriminates against a member of the bargaining unit on the basis of race violates not only its duty of fair representation, but also the

Section 8(b)(1)(A) prohibition against restraint and coercion of employees. The union may be stripped of its certification and ordered to cease and desist the unlawful practices (56 LRRM 1289, 63 LRRM 2395, 63 LRRM 2559). The U.S. Court of Appeals for the District of Columbia went even further and held that an employer who discriminates in employment on the basis of race violates Section 8(a)(1) of the Act. (70 LRRM 2489)

Occupational Safety and Health Act—In 1970, Congress adopted the Occupational Safety and Health Act—one of the most comprehensive laws affecting labor-management relations. Its coverage extends to over 57 million employees—all those whose activities affect interstate commerce. Basically, it requires employers and employees to comply with safety and health standards promulgated by the Labor Department. There are stringent penalties for violations.

THE STATE LABOR LAWS

A substantial proportion of the states also have laws relating to the conduct of labor-management relations or the activities of labor unions. Some preceded the federal statutes; others followed the adoption of the federal laws and were patterned after them. A number of states, for example, have little Norris-LaGuardia Acts limiting the jurisdicton of state courts to issue injunctions in labor disputes. Others have little Wagner or Taft-Hartley Acts. There also are the state fair employment practice laws, right-to-work laws forbidding all forms of union-security contracts, and laws restricting the rights of unions to strike or picket, although many of the restrictions on strikes or picketing have been invalidated by judicial holdings.

Whenever a state law covers an area also regulated by a federal statute, problems of exclusive or concurrent jurisdiction and federal preemption arise. The 1959 amendment to the Taft-Hartley Act, giving the states authority to handle cases rejected by the NLRB under its jurisdictional standards, resolved one of the most difficult of these problems. But others still remain.

About 40 of the states also have fair employment practice laws, while 70 governments have human relations ordinances.

WHAT BOOKLET DOES

Most of the rules governing the conduct of labor relations discussed in this booklet stem from the National Labor Relations Act, as amended in 1947 and 1959. Others are based on the Landrum-Griffith Act, the Norris-LaGuardia Act, or the common law. References given in parentheses are to volume and page of Labor Relations Reference Manual, cited as LRRM; Labor Arbitration Reports, cited as LA; Wage and Hour Cases, cited as WH Cases; or Fair Employment Practice Cases, cited as FEP Cases. Statutory references are to pages in Labor Relations Expediter, cited as LRX. All are published by The Bureau of National Affairs, Inc., Washington, D.C.

When the term Labor Board or merely Board is used without further qualification, it refers to the National Labor Relations Board. The abbreviation NLRB also is used for this agency.

WHO IS COVERED BY THE LAW

Whether a particular worker, union, or employer is covered by the provisions of the Taft-Hartley Act depends on the statutory definitions of the terms "interstate commerce," "employer," and "employee." But even if a worker qualifies as an "employee" and his employer's activities are such as to bring him within the coverage of the Act, the employee still may not be able to get his case before the NLRB. The NLRB limits the cases it will accept by use of a series of jurisdictional standards. These standards are based on the dollar volume of goods the employer buys from or ships to other states or the annual dollar volume of business he does.

TEST OF 'AFFECTING COMMERCE'

It was the intention of Congress to extend the application of the Act to the farthest reaches of interstate commerce. The test is whether the employer's activities "affect" interstate commerce. Except in the District of Columbia, where all commerce is covered, the commerce "affected" must be such as crosses state lines.

But this does not mean that products must be shipped across state lines. It is sufficient that raw materials, power, or communications used cross state lines. Potentially, therefore, the NLRB is given the authority to exercise its jurisdiction over all but the smallest of businesses.

The NLRB, however, has never exercised its broad statutory grant of jurisdiction to the fullest. It has used its administrative discretion to fix limits beyond which it will not tread. Since 1950, it has done this by application of a set of jurisdictional yardsticks.

In 1958, the Board revised these standards in such a way as to lay the basis for the broadest assertion of jurisdiction it ever had exercised. For a manufacturing company, for example, the test was $50,000 annual receipts from or shipments to other states. For retail firms, the test was $500,000 gross annual volume of business. Moreover, the 1959 amendments to the law forbid the Board ever to change the standards in such a way as to reduce the number of cases it will accept. See LRX 373 for the standards for the various categories of business.

The NLRB, however, has expanded its jurisdiction in some areas under the concept of jurisdictional standards. In the Butte Hospital and University Nursing Home cases, it asserted jurisdiction over private proprietary hospitals and nursing homes that meet specified dollar-volume standards. (66 LRRM 1299, 66 LRRM 1268) Then in the Cornell case, it asserted jurisdiction over private, nonprofit colleges and universities. It later established dollar-volume standards for such jurisdiction. (74 LRRM 1269, 75 LRRM 1442) In 1974, Congress amended the Act to give the NLRB jurisdiction over private nonprofit hospitals and nursing homes.

WHO IS AN 'EMPLOYEE'

The Act's definition of an "employee" includes not only persons currently on an employer's payroll but also persons whose work has ceased because of a current strike or an unfair labor practice and who have not obtained other regular and substantially equivalent employment. The following workers, however, are specifically exempted:

▶ Agricultural laborers.

▶ Persons employed in the domestic service of a family or person at his home.

▶ Individuals employed by spouse or parents.

▶ Independent contractors.

▶ Supervisory employees.

▶ Persons employed by employers subject to the Railway Labor Act.

The most important of these exceptions is that relating to supervisors. Prior to the 1947 Taft-Hartley amendments, supervisors were not excluded from the definition of "employee," and the employer could not discriminate against them for engaging in union activity. Since 1947, however, supervisors have not been protected by the Act. Supervisors still may join unions, if they so wish, but they also may be discharged for doing so, and there is nothing in the law that compels an employer to deal with any union they may designate to represent them (23 LRRM 1242). If, however, the effect of a supervisor's discharge is to intimidate nonsupervisory employees in the exercise of their rights under the Act, the NLRB may find a violation and order reinstatement (40 LRRM 2027).

Included in the category of supervisors are those who have authority to hire and discharge, to adjust grievances, to make effective recommendations in such matters, or responsibly to direct their subordinates. The NLRB has held that the last attribute—responsibly to direct other employees—is sufficient to classify an employee as a "supervisor," even if all other marks of supervisory status are lacking. (23 LRRM 1242)

Although nothing in the Act excludes "confidential" or "managerial" workers from the definition of "employee," there have been NLRB and court decisions that have excluded them because of their access to employment and labor relations records and files in the case of confidential employees and their functions in formulating and executing management decisions in the case of managerial employees. (77 LRRM 2561, 77 LRRM 3114)

In a decision handed down in late 1971, the Supreme Court held that retirees no longer are "employees" within the meaning of the Act. So it cleared Pittsburgh Plate Glass Co. of refusal-to-bargain charges based on its unilateral modification of the benefits of retired employees. (78 LRRM 2974) Although not required to bargain about changes in the benefits of retirees, many companies still do on a voluntary basis.

WHO IS AN 'EMPLOYER'

In addition to employers whose operations do not affect interstate commerce, the Act exempts from its jurisdiction the following groups of employers:

▶ The Federal Government or any wholly owned government corporation or any federal reserve bank.

▶ Any state or political division of a state.

▶ Employers subject to the Railway Labor Act.

▶ Labor organizations, except when acting as employers.

The liability of an employer for actions that may violate the Act extends to the acts of the employer's "agents." This means, for one thing, that an employer may be held responsible for what one of his supervisors does as long as the supervisor was acting in his line of duty. This will be so even though the supervisor may not have been authorized to perform the particular act. But an employer normally is not charged with responsibility for isolated or sporadic instances of anti-union conduct by his supervisors, at least where there has been no approval of the conduct by the employer. (23 LRRM 2197)

EMPLOYEES' ORGANIZING RIGHTS

The rights of employees to organize into labor organizations and to bargain collectively with their employers are two of the basic rights guaranteed under the Act. To insure the free exercise of these rights, the Act makes certain actions by employers and unions unfair labor practices. It thus establishes ground rules for the conduct of organizing activities.

These rules drastically restrict what an employer may do once an organizing drive is under way. He may not restrain, coerce, or interfere with employees in the exercise of their rights under the law; he may not discriminate against employees because of their union activities or membership or because of their refusal to engage in such activities or to join the union; he may not dominate or assist a labor organization; and he may not refuse to recognize and bargain with a union duly selected to represent his employees.

WHAT IS 'INTERFERENCE'

The unfair labor practice of "interference" is a broad one, embracing the more specific unfair practices of discrimination, domination, and refusal to bargain, plus a variety of additional acts. The acts forbidden range all the way from restraining the solicitation of union members to granting a wage increase during an organizing drive.

Suppose a union begins distributing literature and soliciting members in a plant. What restrictions may the employer lawfully place on the distribution and solicitation? The NLRB has laid down some specific rules on this. The important considerations are these: Who is doing the soliciting or distribution, employees or outside organizers; where it takes place, on or off company property; and when it takes place, within or outside working time.

In brief, these are the rules:

▶ An employer may ban outside (nonemployee) union organizers from distributing or soliciting on company property, except where the employees may not reasonably be reached otherwise or where the ban is applied discriminatorily against the union. Outside organizers, for example, were held to have a right to distribute literature within an industrial park where the employees could not be reached by reasonable efforts using other available means and the no-distribution rule was applied discriminatorily only against unions. (68 LRRM 1385) But the Supreme Court later stressed that the right of outside union organizers to solicit and distribute literature on an employer's property still was governed by the rules laid down in the 1956 Babcock & Wilcox Co. case. (38 LRRM 2001) These are (1) whether the union may reach the employees through other available channels, and (2) whether the employer's order discriminates against the union by allowing other solicitation or distribution.

Two later cases brought these rules into sharp focus. In a case decided solely on the constitutional issue of free speech, the U.S. Supreme Court held that a Pennsylvania court violated the U.S. Constitution by enjoining a union's picketing in a pickup zone and parking lot in a shopping center. There were five opinions by the Court. This was the Logan Valley Plaza case. (68 LRRM 2209)

In a follow-up case, the U.S. Court of Appeals for the Eighth Circuit tried to apply the Logan Valley rationale to a case arising under the Taft-Hartley Act to forbid the enforcement of no-solicitation rules by outside union organizers on a shopping center's parking lots. But the Supreme Court said this was incorrect. Logan Valley involved a constitutional issue. In Taft-Hartley cases, the Court stressed, the Babcock & Wilcox test still applies—whether other reasonable means of communication with the employees were available to the outside union organizers. (80 LRRM 2769)

▶ An employer normally also may prohibit his employees from engaging in union solicitation or distribution of literature during their working time both in the working and nonworking areas of the plant. As one judge said, "working time is for work." Moreover, an employer may forbid his employees to distribute literature in working areas even during their nonworking time. (51 LRRM 1110)

▶ The NLRB later laid down specific rules involving "area" tests for determining the legality of no-distribution and no-solicitation rules. It held: (1) A rule forbidding distribution of union literature by employees in working areas will be presumptively valid even though it applies both to working and nonworking time; (2) a rule forbidding distribution on nonworking time in nonworking areas will be presumptively invalid; (3) a rule forbidding union solicitation by employees during their nonworking time will be presumptively invalid even though limited to working areas; and (4) a rule forbidding union solicitation during working time in any plant area will be presumptively valid. (51 LRRM 1110)

▶ There are exceptions where there are special circumstances making stricter rules necessary to maintain production or discipline. An example of such special circumstances is a retail store, in which solicitation may be forbidden in selling areas even during the employees' nonworking time. (57 LRRM 1110, 45 LRRM 1370, 29 LRRM 1305)

▶ If, however, a retail store enforces a broad no-solicitation rule forbidding union solicitation on the selling floors during both the working and nonworking time of the employees, officials of the store may not make speeches to "captive" audiences of employees on company time and property before a representation election unless the union is given an equal opportunity to reply. This is the so-called captive-audience rule, first enunciated by the NLRB in the Bonwit-Teller case and then revived in the 1962 May Department Store decision. Such captive-audience speeches are considered both an unfair labor practice and grounds for setting an election aside, although at least one U.S. court of appeals does not agree with this holding. (49 LRRM 1862, 53 LRRM 2172)

▶ An incumbent union may not waive the rights of employees to distribute literature to co-workers in nonworking areas during nonworking time or to engage in in-plant solicitation on nonworking time. There had been a division of opinion on this issue, but the Supreme Court adopted the view that such a waiver would freeze out organizational efforts on behalf of a rival union. (85 LRRM 2475)

Many other types of employer conduct have been held unlawful interference under the Act. The following are a few examples:

Questioning of Employees—For many years, the NLRB held that an employer's questioning of employees about their union activities or those of fellow employees of itself amounted to unlawful interference. The Board modified this position twice—first in 1954 and again in 1967. Under the current policy, an employer's polling of employees as to their union views will be considered unlawful, in the absence of unusual circumstances, unless (1) the purpose of the poll is to determine the truth of a union's claim of majority status; (2) the employees are told that this is the purpose of the poll; (3) assurance against reprisal is given; (4) the employees are polled by secret ballot; and (5) the employer has not engaged in unfair labor practices or otherwise created a coercive atmosphere. The Board emphasized the importance that the polling be done by secret ballot as giving further assurance "that reprisals cannot be taken against employees because the views of each individual will not be known." (34 LRRM 1384, 65 LRRM 1386)

In a 1972 case, the Board ordered an employer to bargain with a union where the employer conducted a private poll of all the employees in the bargaining unit and learned that a majority of them had signed authorization cards stating that they wanted the union to represent them in collective bargaining. Only Member Kennedy of the five-member Board dissented. The majority said that the employer could not reject the results of his privately conducted poll. (81 LRRM 1313) A similar ruling was made in a case in which there were only four employees in the unit and the employer had independent knowledge of the union's majority. (74 LRRM 1113)

Closing or Moving the Plant—An employer has an absolute right to close his entire business for any reason he chooses, including anti-union bias. But he does not have such a right to close part of his business, to transfer work to another plant, or to open a new plant to replace a closed plant if the partial closing is motivated by a purpose to "chill" unionism in the remaining parts of the business and the employer reasonably can foresee that it will have that effect. This was the Darlington holding. If the employer's decision to move or partially to close is based solely on economic considerations, there is no violation, although there may be an obligation to bargain about the decision and its effects (58 LRRM 2657, 65 LRRM 1391). Moreover, an employer was held not to have violated the Act by closing part of his business where the closure was a result of the employer's religious conviction against dealing with a union and not the result of any desire to chill unionism in the remaining parts of the business. (64 LRRM 1321)

In a decision indicating a change in viewpoint resulting from the appointment of new members to the Board, the NLRB ruled that an employer did not violate the Act by failing to bargain with the union about a decision to close part of his operations where the decision involved a major change in the nature of the employer's business. (79 LRRM 1396) In so ruling, the Board accepted the doctrine enunciated by the U.S. Courts of Appeals for the Third and Eighth Circuits that where a major business decision is involved, the employer is required to bargain with the union only about the effects of the decision on employees and not about the decision itself. (60 LRRM 2033, 60 LRRM 2084) The Board previously had rejected this doctrine. (63 LRRM 1264)

In a similar holding, the Ninth Circuit Court of Appeals held that an employer was not required to bargain about a decision based solely on greatly changed economic conditions to terminate his business and reinvest the capital in a different enterprise in another location as a minority partner. A decision of such fundamental importance to the basic direction of the corporate enterprise, the court said, is not included within the area of mandatory bargaining under the Act. (65 LRRM 2861)

Anti-Union Petitions—The Act permits an employer to express noncoercive opinions of unions, but it does not permit him to inject himself directly into the business of getting employees to withdraw from a union. Circulating an anti-union petition may result in the employer's being found guilty of interference. (24 LRRM 1317)

Increases in Wages and Other Benefits—Unilateral increases in wages or other benefits during a union organizing campaign have been regarded as a prime form of unlawful interference even though granted permanently and unconditionally. The same is true of a promise by the employer to increase wages or other benefits at a "crucial" time during a union organizing drive. There is an exception, however, where all the employer does is put into effect a regularly scheduled increase or one that had been decided upon and announced before the organizing campaign began. In fact, a delay or denial of a regularly scheduled increase during an organizing campaign might itself be unlawful interference. (14 LRRM 581, 30 LRRM 2046, 30 LRRM 1154, 30 LRRM 2305, 55 LRRM 2098)

Removal of Privileges—The removal of privileges enjoyed by employees or threats to take privileges away will constitute illegal interference where the object is to discourage union organization. (31 LRRM 2082)

Espionage and Surveillance—Although the use of "labor spies" is now a rarity, there have been a number of cases in which employers have been found to have engaged in unlawful interference by surveillance of their employees' union activities. The general rule is that any real check or guard maintained by management over union meetings or other union activities constitutes illegal interference "whether frankly open or carefully concealed." (15 LRRM 826)

Threat or Prediction—The courts have distinguished between a threat of retaliation for joining a union and a mere "prediction" of what may happen if a union won an election. Such a "prediction" may not be unlawful. (66 LRRM 2707)

Anti-Union Movie—An employer's showing of the movie "And Women Must Weep" as part of an orientation program for employees was not unlawful interference under the Act, but was an exercise of free speech protected by Section 8 (c) of the Act. The Fifth Circuit Court of Appeals said that the employer could not be found guilty of an unfair labor practice unless the showing of the film amounted to a "threat of reprisal or force." The movie, which purports to be a true account of a 1956 strike at an Indiana plant, admittedly shows the bad side of unionism and is designed to discourage union membership. The court's decision reversed that of the NLRB. (65 LRRM 3042) The Eighth Circuit Court of Appeals similarly reversed a Board holding that the showing of the movie was unlawful interference. (70 LRRM 2193) The Board had relied on earlier decisions holding that the showing of the movie was ground for setting a representation election aside. (51 LRRM 1558, 53 LRRM 1063)

UNLAWFUL DISCRIMINATION

It is an unfair labor practice under Section 8(a)(3) of the Act for an employer to encourage or discourage union membership by discrimination with regard to hire or tenure of employment. It also is an unfair labor practice under Section 8(a)(4) for an employer to discharge or otherwise discriminate against an employee because he has filed charges or given testimony under the Act.

This does not mean that an employer may not discharge or otherwise discriminate against an employee for other reasons. As one court put it, an employee "may be discharged by the employer for a good reason, a poor reason, or no reason at all, so long as the terms of the statute are not violated." (10 LRRM 483)

In determining whether an employer's discriminatory action encouraged or discouraged union membership, the NLRB and the courts look at a number of factors—the motive of the employer, his knowledge or lack of knowledge of the union activity, and his attitude toward unionization. "Subjective evidence" that the employees actually were encouraged or discouraged in their attitudes toward the union isn't required. Where a natural consequence of the discrimination is encouragement or discouragement of union membership, it is presumed that the employer intended such consequences. Moreover, some acts, such as a grant of superseniority to strikers' replacements or grant of accrued vacation to replacements but not strikers, are regarded as so inherently discriminatory as to be unlawful without regard to the employer's motive. (33 LRRM 2417, 2438; 53 LRRM 2121, 65 LRRM 2465)

In specific cases, the NLRB and the courts have considered such factors as the following in determining whether an employer's motive in discharging or otherwise disciplining employees was to encourage or discourage union membership:

Knowledge of Union Activity—To establish that an employee was discriminatorily discharged because of his union activities, it must be shown that the employer had knowledge of those activities. But in such cases, a supervisor's knowledge of the employee's activities will be imputed to the employer. (28 LRRM 1351)

Anti-Union Background—If considerations appear more or less evenly balanced, the Board and the courts often will look for guidance to the employer's background attitude toward unions or employee organization. But the Board and the courts also may consider the lack of evidence of a "legitimate and substantial business justification" for the employer's action. (17 LRRM 781, 31 LRRM 1607, 65 LRRM 2465)

Unequal Enforcement of Plant Rules—If an employer discharges a union adherent for violating a rule that has not been enforced with respect to other employees, the Board may consider this evidence that the discharge was discriminatorily motivated. This would not be so if the employer could show that the rule had been applied uniformly to all employers. (28 LRRM 1075, 30 LRRM 2101)

Timing of Discharge—The Board always looks with suspicion on the discharge or layoff of an employee immediately after the employer has learned of the employee's participation in union activity. In such a case, the Board will scrutinize closely the reason alleged by the employer as causing the discharge. (29 LRRM 2379)

Questioning and Surveillance—If an employer has questioned an employee about his union membership or has asked someone to watch and see whether he attends union meetings, the employer already will have two strikes against him if he discharges the employee and charges of discrimination are filed. (31 LRRM 2082)

Retaliation for Union Activity—In one of the rare cases involving the Section 8(a)(4) prohibition against an employer's discrimination against an employee for engaging in union activity, the U.S. Supreme Court unanimously held that an employer violated the Act by discharging employees because they had given sworn statements to an NLRB field examiner who was investigating an unfair-labor-practice charge filed against the employer. The U.S. Court of Appeals for the Sixth Circuit had held that Section 8(a)(4) protects an employee against reprisal only for *filing* an unfair-labor-practice charge or for giving testimony at a formal hearing. But the Supreme Court said that to protect an employee during the investigative stage of a proceeding is consistent with the legislative purpose of the Act. This is necessary, it added, "to present the Board's channels of information from being dried up by employer intimidation of prospective complainants." (79 LRRM 2587)

Racial Discrimination—Is it a violation of the Taft-Hartley Act for an employer to discriminate in employment on the basis of race? It has been well established that a union that discriminates on the basis of race violates its duty of fair representation. But in 1969, the U.S. Court of Appeals for the District of Columbia remanded a case to the Board for a determination whether an employer who discriminated on the basis of race or national origin violated the Act. (70 LRRM 2489) The Board avoided the basic issue on remand by finding that there was insufficient evidence of discriminaton based on race in the case. (78 LRRM 1465) Then in 1973, the Board clarified its position on the issue. It held that employment discrimination based on race, color, sex, religion, or national origin, "standing alone," is not inherently destructive of employees' rights under Section 7 of the Act and so does not constitute a *per se* violation of the Act. There must be actual evidence of a connection between the discriminatory conduct and interference with employees' Section 7 rights. (82 LRRM 1483)

REINSTATEMENT AND BACK PAY

Where the NLRB has found that an employee was discharged unlawfully, it ordinarily will order that he be reinstated on unconditional application, even if this means discharging an employee who may have been hired to take his place. In a large proportion of the cases, the Board also will order the employer to make good to the employee any loss of wages he has suffered as a result of the discharge. If a union caused the employer to discharge the employee unlawfully, the back-pay order may be directed against either the union or the employer, or it may be directed against both.

In computing how much back pay is due a discriminatorily discharged employee, the NLRB gives weight to a number of factors —whether the employee has been offered reinstatement and when, whether the business of the employer was such that the employee may not have been employed during the entire period, whether the employee sought other work, whether he had earnings from another job. Here are some of the rules applied:

Terminating Liability—Although the back-pay bill may continue to mount until the employer complies with the order, the employer can terminate the increase at any time by an offer of reinstatement to the employee. If the employee accepts, he begins to draw wages again. If he unequivocally refuses reinstatement, the employer no longer is assessed with additions to the amount to be paid. (6 LRRM 310)

Duty To Seek Work—An employee claiming back pay must have made a reasonable effort to obtain other work. If he fails to do so, the Board will deduct from the back pay the amount of wage losses willfully incurred. Registration with a government employment office will not be regarded as "conclusive proof" of a reasonable search for other work, but will be given greater or less weight depending on all the circumstances of the case. Diligence in making independent applications for jobs and use of other hiring facilities also will be considered. An employee need not, however, accept another job to protect his back pay if it isn't "substantially equivalent" to his former position. (26 LRRM 1189, 38 LRRM 1317)

Offsets Against Back Pay—Where a discriminatorily discharged employee has obtained another job, the amount he earns in that job ordinarily will be deducted from the amount paid to him as back wages. If, however, the employee is put to extra expense to obtain or retain another job—for example, employment agency fees, commuting expenses above those usually incurred, or expenses required by living away from home—the extra expenses will not be deducted in computing "net earnings" at the interim job. (26 LRRM 1189)

What Back Pay Includes—Basically, the back pay awarded to a discriminatorily discharged employee is intended to make him whole for earnings lost as a result of the discharge. As computed by the NLRB, the back pay will include: wage increases that would have been received but for the discharge computed from the date of discharge to the date of an offer of reinstatement (50 LRRM 1042); the increased pay from a promotion that would have been received but for the discharge (28 LRRM 1447); overtime pay that would have been earned but for the discharge (5 LRRM 158); bonuses (29 LRRM 1049); and six percent interest on the total (51 LRRM 1122).

But the back pay will not cover periods when the employee would not have worked even if no discrimination had taken place. These include, for example, a period when the employee would have been laid off for economic reasons if he hadn't been laid off first for discriminatory reasons (28 LRRM 2323). They also include a period of sickness not covered by any sick-leave policy of the employer (26 LRRM 1189).

'Make-Whole' Orders—Closely related to the issue of back pay is whether the NLRB may require an employer who has refused to bargain in good faith to compensate the employees for the wages and benefits they might have obtained if the employer had bargained with their union in good faith. The NLRB has refused to issue such orders. (79 LRRM 1175, 79 LRRM 1693)

See below under "The Duty to Bargain" for a further discussion of this issue.

Remedies in 'Flagrant' Cases—Where the NLRB has found what it terms "flagrant" or "massive" violations, it has ordered remedies that go beyond the usual cease-and-desist order, reinstatement, and back pay. In a series of cases involving J.P. Stevens & Co., for example, the Board ordered the company to take such additional actions as (1) mailing to each of its employees in its North and South Carolina plants, not just those involved in the case, a copy of the cease-and-desist order signed by a company official; (2) giving the union reasonable access to plant bulletin boards for a period of one year; (3) giving the union a list of the names and addresses of the employees of the plants involved; and (4) having the cease-and-desist order read to assembled groups of employees by a Board official. The original orders required that the order be read to employees by a company official and that the union be given the names and addresses of employees in all North and South Carolina plants. These requirements were modified by courts. (61 LRRM 1437, 64 LRRM 1321, 66 LRRM 1024, 66 LRRM 1030, 69 LRRM 1088, 70 LRRM 2104, 72 LRRM 2433, 65 LRRM 2829, 67 LRRM 2055)

ASSISTING OR DOMINATING UNION

In making it an unfair labor practice for an employer to dominate or assist a union, the Labor Relations Act was aiming at the so-called "company union"—a term often used in a derisive sense to indicate a company-dominated union. The NLRB, in its first two decisions under this ban as revised in 1947, held that there were two degrees of violation.

First, there are those cases involving employer's unfair practices that are so extensive as to constitute a domination of the labor organization. In such cases, the NLRB will order disestablishment of the organization, regardless of whether or not it is affiliated with the AFL-CIO. (21 LRRM 1232)

Second, there are those cases in which the unfair practices are limited to support and interference that never reached the point of domination. In these cases, the NLRB will "only order that recognition be withheld until certification, again without regard to whether or not the organization happens to be affiliated." (21 LRRM 1237)

Since whether a union has been dominated or assisted by an employer is a question of degree, no one fact ordinarily is conclusive. The U.S. Supreme Court has said that the "whole congeries of facts" presented to the NLRB may be considered in support of its findings. (7 LRRM 297)

Unlawful support to a union may be either financial or nonfinancial. Where it is financial, the illegality is measured not in terms of its costs to the employer but in terms of its effect upon the recipient organization and the employees. (17 LRRM 176)

Some examples of unlawful *financial* support to a union are:

▶ Payment of employee representatives for time spent in committee meetings. (29 LRRM 2112)

▶ Loans to defray union expenses. (29 LRRM 1054)

▶ Furnishing free office space or facilities. (6 LRRM 684)

▶ Permitting the union's operation of vending machines or concessions. (29 LRRM 1051)

Some examples of unlawful *nonfinancial* support to a union are:

▶ Permitting use of company time and property for organizational or other union activities. (6 LRRM 684)

▶ Recognition of, or execution of a contract with, the union without requiring proof of its majority status. There is, however, a special provision that permits an employer "primarily in the building and construction industry" to execute a contract with a union before it has established its majority status. (24 LRRM 2409)

▶ Falsely crediting the union with obtaining wage increases or other employee benefits. (24 LRRM 2409)

▶ Signing a contract with a union at a time when the number of employees at work is not representative of the planned work force. (40 LRRM 1344)

RESTRICTIONS ON UNIONS

The 1947 Taft-Hartley Act and the 1959 Landrum-Griffin Act placed restrictions on what a union may do in its efforts to organize employees. These restrictions are discussed later in the chapter on "Strikes, Picketing, and Boycotts."

EMPLOYER LOCKOUTS

For a discussion of the rules governing the use of the employer's lockout weapon, see below under "Strikes, Picketing, Boycotts, and Lockouts."

CHOOSING A BARGAINING AGENT

A basic objective of the Labor Relations Act is to protect the right of employees to bargain collectively with their employer through a representative of their own choosing. This does not mean that each little group of organized employees may name its spokesman. Instead, the Act provides that all employees in an appropriate unit, whether members of the union or not, are to be represented by the organization that is chosen by the majority. And the Act establishes election machinery for choosing a majority representative.

Prior to the 1959 amendments to the Taft-Hartley Act, the NLRB itself decided whether and when an election should be held, what employees should be permitted to vote, and whether an election had been conducted under such circumstances as to ensure a free choice by the employees. The amendments, however, gave the Board power to delegate decision-making authority in election cases to its regional directors.

Exercising this authority, the Board gave its regional directors the power to handle the ordinary representation election and post-election challenges and objections. The regional directors also may rule on employer election petitions, decertification petitions, and requests for elections to rescind a union's authority to negotiate union-security contracts.

The Board, however, retained authority to rule on election issues where there is a stipulation for certification upon a consent election and on objections and challenges arising from elections to rescind a union's authority to make union-security contracts. In all other cases, the regional director's decision on preelection and post-election issues is final unless review is granted by the Board.

WHO MAY ASK FOR ELECTION

A petition for a representation election may be filed by an employee, a group of employees, a union, or an employer. These are the rules:

Union Petition—A union may petition for an election where either (1) it is seeking recognition as exclusive bargaining agent and the employer refuses to recognize it, or (2) it has been recognized but wants an election to obtain the benefits of a certification. (23 LRRM 1022, 23 LRRM 1589)—

Except where an "expedited" election is sought under the provisions relating to recognition or organizational picketing, discussed below, the petition should be accompained by proof that at least 30 percent of the employees in the unit are interested in having the union represent them.

Individual Petitions—An election petition filed by an individual, like one filed by a union, must be backed by a 30-percent showing of interest among the employees. Other than this, the individual need show only that he is seeking representative status for the purpose of collective bargaining. A petition may not, however, be filed by a supervisor. Since a supervisor may not represent employees for bargaining purposes, the NLRB will dismiss petitions filed by supervisors. (29 LRRM 1300)

Employer Petitions—Except where the union is engaging in organizational or recognition picketing, an employer may petition for a representation election only if he is confronted with a demand by the union for exclusive bargaining recognition.

A formal request for recognition is not required, however. The Board will direct an election even if it is claimed that the employer has no reasonable basis for questioning the union's majority. (25 LRRM 1039)

Other unions may be permitted to intervene in an election if they can show some interest in it—an existing contract with the employer, for example. They need not make a 30-percent showing of interest, however.

PETITIONS IN PICKETING CASES

A new Section 8(b)(7)(C) inserted in the Taft Act by the Landrum-Griffin amendments makes it unlawful for a union to picket for recognition or organizational purposes if no election petition is filed within a reasonable period of time (not to exceed 30 days).

But when a petition is filed in one of these cases, the NLRB must direct an election "forthwith" without regard to the usual requirements that (1) an employer petition be based on a demand for recognition by the union, (2) a union petition be based on a 30-percent showing of interest among the employees, and (3) the Board first conduct an investigation and hearing.

This section of the law is discussed in more detail in the chapter on "Strikes, Picketing, Boycotts, and Lockouts."

DETERMINING BARGAINING UNIT

Subject to certain limitations, the Labor Management Relations Act confers on the NLRB the authority to determine in each case what the appropriate bargaining unit shall be. This could be, for example, an employer-wide unit, a plant unit, a craft unit, or a departmental unit.

The 1947 Taft-Hartley amendments, however, placed some express limitations on the NLRB's authority in the determination of bargaining units. These include:

▶ The extent to which employees have organized a union shall not be controlling. If, for example, a union has organized one department of a plant or a part of a department, the NLRB may not direct an election among those particular employees just because the union has not been able to organize employees elsewhere in the plant. Extent of organization, however, may be one of several factors considered by the Board to justify a certain unit. (58 LRRM 2721)

▶ Professional employees may not be included in a unit with nonprofessionals unless a majority of the professional employees vote for this inclusion in a separate self-determination election.

▶ Plant guards may not be included in a unit of production and maintenance workers. The only appropriate unit covering plant guards is one that is limited exclusively to plant guards. Furthermore, a plant guard union may not be certified if it takes persons other than guards into membership or is affiliated, directly or indirectly, with a union that represents persons other than guards.

▶ In ruling on requests for a unit of skilled craftsmen and their helpers and apprentices to be severed from a broader unit, the Board is limited by a craft-unit proviso to Section 9 of the Act. (Craft-severance elections are discussed in more detail below.)

PERSONS EXCLUDED FROM UNIT

In addition to these limitations on the Board's authority to determine appropriate bargaining units, the Act requires that certain types of employees be excluded from the unit regardless of the type of unit. The principal class of exclusions consists of persons identified with management's interests. Apart from supervisory employees, who are excluded by statute, the Board customarily excludes buyer-salesmen (42 LRRM 1450) and stockholders who are members of the company's board of directors (41 LRRM 1521).

Also excluded are (1) confidential employees "who assist and act in a confidential capacity to persons who formulate, determine, and effectuate management policies in the field of labor relations," (2) children and spouse of the employer; (3) "managerial"employees who formulate and execute policies of the employer; (4) temporary employees, including students hired during school vacations; and (5) retired employees or persons drawing social security annuities. But regular part-time employees are not excluded, nor are employees on vacation, sick leave, or other authorized leave of absence. Moreover, no "managerial employee" is within the scope of the Act. The Supreme Court rejected the NLRB's view that only those in positions susceptible to conflicts of interests if unionized should be excluded from the Act. (85 LRRM 2945) In another case involving a unit of taxicab drivers, the Board included 115 drivers who, along with 27 ex-drivers, made up the company's stockholders. (77 LRRM 1376)

Working within these statutory limitations, the NLRB has developed some tests of its own for determining appropriate bargaining units. One basic principle it has laid down is that the unit determined need not be the *only* appropriate unit, or the *ultimate* unit, or the *most* appropriate unit. It is necessary only that the unit be "appropriate." Thus, the Board sometimes finds that alternate units are appropriate and lets the employees determine which unit they approve in so-called self-determination elections.

Among the principal factors the Board considers in determining whether particular units are appropriate are the following:

▶ The similarity of duties, skills, wages, and working conditions of the employees involved.

▶ The pertinent collective bargaining history, if any, among the employees involved. Also, in some instances, the history, extent, and type of union organization in other plants of the same company or the same industry.

▶ The extent and type of union organization of the employees involved, although the Board is forbidden by the statute to make the extent of organization the controlling factor.

▶ The employees' own wishes in the matter. This refers only to those cases involving professional employees, employees with certain craft skills, and certain other groups where the Board permits employees to vote separately on the question of whether they should be placed in a unit limited to their own group or placed in a larger unit. These are called self-determination elections.

► The appropriateness of the units proposed in relation to the organizational structure of the company itself.

CRAFT, DEPARTMENTAL UNITS

Under Section 9(b) of the Act, the NLRB is forbidden to "decide that any craft unit is inappropriate * * * on the ground that a different unit has been established by a prior Board determination, unless a majority of the employees in the proposed craft unit vote against separate representation."

National Tube Decision—In its 1948 National Tube Decision, the Board appeared to give this proviso only limited significance. It construed the proviso as not barring it from considering prior determinations and bargaining history as long as neither was made the sole ground for the decision.

On this basis, the Board decided that craft-severance elections should not be directed in the basic steel industry in view of the integrated nature of operations in the industry and the history of bargaining on an industrial, rather than craft, basis (21 LRRM 1292). This policy of denying craft-severance elections later was extended to three other "integrated" industries—wet milling, lumber, and aluminum (23 LRRM 1090, 25 LRRM 1173, 26 LRRM 1039).

American Potash Decision—In the 1954 American Potash case, the Board took a new look at the craft-severance problem and changed its policy. It decided that henceforth craft units must be split off from an established industrial unit whenever (1) the unit sought to be severed is a "true craft group," and (2) the union seeking severance traditionally has represented employees in the craft. But the Board did rule that it would not permit craft severance in the four industries covered by the National Tube doctrine. (33 LRRM 1380)

Mallinckrodt Chemical Decision—Then in 1966, the Board decided to revise its rules on craft-severance elections completely. Henceforth, the Board said, it will consider all areas relevant to an informed decision in craft-severance cases, including the following: (1) whether the proposed unit embraces a distinct and homogeneous group of skilled craftsmen performing the functions of their craft on a nonrepetitive basis; (2) the bargaining history of employees and the plant and other plants of the employer; (3) the extent to which the employees have maintained their separate identity during their inclusion in the broader unit; (4) the history and pattern of bargaining in the industry; (5) the degree of integration of the employer's production processes; (6) the qualifications of the union seeking to represent a severed unit. Both the American Potash and the National Tube decisions were revised in accordance with these principles. (64 LRRM 1011)

INSURANCE, RETAIL UNITS

Prior to 1969, the NLRB permitted only state-wide or employer-wide bargaining units of employees of insurance companies. But in the next few years, the Board began determining that smaller units were appropriate for bargaining. It was upheld in these determinations by the Third, Fourth, and Sixth Circuit Courts of Appeals, but reversed by the First Circuit, and this case was taken to the Supreme Court. The Supreme Court remanded the case to the Board to articulate its reasons for determining the smaller units and to show that "extent of organization" was not the *sole* reason. This the Board did in its decision on the remand. (53 LRRM 2519, 55 LRRM 2448, 55 LRRM 2930, 55 LRRM 2444, 58 LRRM 2721, 61 LRRM 1249)

The same trend developed in retail chains and department stores, with the Board determining single stores in a chain and single departments in a department store as appropriate units for bargaining. Despite some reversals by Circuit Courts of Appeals, the Board maintained its position that single-store units are presumptively appropriate in retail chains. (51 LRRM 1152, 56 LRRM 1246, 60 LRRM 2234, 65 LRRM 2261, 66 LRRM 2507, 68 LRRM 1497)

In a series of cases involving department stores in the New York area, the Board departed from its prior policy that a store-wide unit was the optimum unit and held that separate units of selling, nonselling, restaurant, and clerical employees were appropriate under some circumstances. (58 LRRM 1081, 58 LRRM 1086, 58 LRRM 1088)

There was an indication in 1972, however, that the Board might start moving back in the other direction. With the three Nixon appointees making up the majority, the Board refused to direct an election in a single store of a retail drug chain. Instead, it held that the appropriate unit should include all of the chain's stores in two counties of Florida. (80 LRRM 1449)

UNITS IN OTHER INDUSTRIES

In cases involving appropriate units in other industries, the NLRB and the courts have made the following rulings:

Nursing Homes—Licensed practical nurses were included in a unit of all employees working at a nursing home. The practical nurses were not considered professional employees within the meaning of the Act. (83 LRRM 1337)

Guard Service, Detective Operations—A unit composed of employees at three offices of an administrative district of a nationwide guard-service and detective company was not considered appropriate. The unit, the Board said, should be districtwide, in view of the centrally determined labor policy, the close supervision from the home office, and the uniform working conditions. (74 LRRM 2355)

University Faculties—A unit of full-time and adjunct faculty members, librarians, research associates, and guidance counselors at a center operated by a private nonprofit university was considered appropriate. These employees were considered "professional employees" under the Act. (77 LRRM 1006) In another case, department chairmen were included in the same unit with faculty members, but a separate unit limited to members of the faculty of the law school was found appropriate. (78 LRRM 1177) In a second case involving a unit of members of a law school faculty, the assistant dean was included in the unit. (84 LRRM 1403)

Warehouses—A unit consisting of employees at one of three warehouses in which a company engages in wholesale operations was found appropriate. A contention that the unit should include all employees engaged in wholesale operations was rejected in view of the separate supervision, minimal transfer and exchange of employees among the three warehouses, and the differences in employee functions. (69 LRRM 1466)

NAMES AND ADDRESSES RULE

As part of its direction of election, the NLRB may require the employer to provide a list of the names and addresses of all employees eligible to vote in the election. The Board then gives the list to the union or any other party to the election.

The Board's authority to require an employer to provide such a list was upheld by the Supreme Court in the Wyman-Gordon case. The Court said that the Board's direction to supply the list of names and addresses was an order the company was obligated to obey. (70 LRRM 3345)

CLARIFICATION OF UNIT

In a controversial decision handed down in 1969, a three-to-two majority of the Board held that it had authority to direct self-determination elections at two of a company's plants to determine whether the employees wanted to continue to be represented separately by a union or to be represented by the same union in a certified multiplant unit that would be company-wide. The majority was composed of Chairman McCulloch and Members Brown and Zagoria; Members Fanning and Jenkins dissented, contending that the Board had no authority to conduct such elections on a petition for clarification of the unit. By a two-to-one margin, the U.S. Court of Appeals for the District of Columbia upheld the Board's decision, and the Supreme Court denied review. (67 LRRM 1096, 68 LRRM 2447, 70 LRRM 2225)

In a later case Member Zagoria appeared to change his position, and the Board dismissed a union's petition to (1) amend a certification to combine four bargaining units, or (2) "clarify" the unit by holding self-determination elections at three plants to determine whether the employees wanted to be represented in the multiplant unit sought by the union. Since the unit sought by the union in this case would not have been company-wide, Zagoria said, it could not be found appropriate on any basis other than agreement of the parties. (73 LRRM 1001)

CONDUCTING THE ELECTION

If the unit sought in the petition is not appropriate, the NLRB regional director will not go ahead with the election. He also will not hold an election on the petition of one union if the employer has a current and valid contract with another union. This contract-bar doctrine and its exceptions are discussed later in this chapter.

Assuming there are no bargaining-unit or contract-bar issues, the regional director will set the machinery for holding the election into motion. If the parties are in agreement, the election will be a consent election and informal procedures will be used. If there is no agreement, the election will be directed after a hearing.

The particular day selected for the election usually will be one when substantially all eligible employees will have a chance to vote. And the voting hours will be arranged so that all eligible voters on all shifts will have adequate opportunity to vote.

The location of the polling places is determined with a view to their easy accessibility to the voters. The Board's regional director usually tries to have the election conducted on company property. He has discretion to determine whether mail ballots should be used.

Official notices of the election are posted in the plant several days before the election. An employer's failure to post the notices may be reason to set the election aside (37 LRRM 1194). However, an employer may not invalidate an election by refusing to post notices. Board agents will undertake to publicize the election under such circumstances (38 LRRM 1124).

The notice of election usually contains a sample copy of the ballot. Defacement or marking of the posted sample ballots is no reason for the Board to set aside the election, unless one of the parties is responsible for the defacement. (40 LRRM 1009)

PREELECTION PROPAGANDA

The Board repeatedly has said that it generally will not censor or police the preelection propaganda of the parties. But it has imposed limitations on such campaign techniques as (1) reproduction of the official ballot, (2) false propaganda, (3) speechmaking immediately before the election, and (4) racial appeals that are not truthful and germane.

Here are some of the rules:

▶ The Board will not permit the distribution of sample ballots marked in favor of "no union" or in favor of one of the competing unions. Only copies of the ballot that are completely unaltered and that are marked "sample" are permissible. The Board will set aside the results of any election where it finds this rule was violated. (34 LRRM 1538)

▶ Although the Board generally leaves it to the good sense of the voters to appraise and evaluate preelection propaganda and to the opposing parties the task of correcting inaccurate and untruthful statements, it will set aside the election if the propaganda has been so presented and timed that the ability of the employees to evaluate it has been impaired to the point that their uncoerced desires cannot be determined. "Inartistic" or "vague" wording, however, will not be sufficient to establish such misrepresentation. (35 LRRM 1035, 51 LRRM 1600)

▶ Both employers and unions are prohibited from making election speeches to massed assemblies of employees on company time within 24 hours before the election is to begin. (33 LRRM 1151)

▶ A retail store that forbids union solicitation in selling areas during both the employees' working and nonworking time must give the union equal opportunity to reply to any speech by an official of the store on company time and property. (49 LRRM 1862)

► Irrelevant and inflammatory racial appeals that are neither truthful nor germane to the election issues will be grounds for setting an election aside. (50 LRRM 1532, 1535)

► Electioneering in and around the polls is ground for setting the election aside. In most cases, the Board will fix a "no-electioneering" area which usually will be a circle with a radius of 100 feet around the polling place. (67 LRRM 1395)

► Threats of retaliation against employees if they vote for the union or promises of benefits if they vote against it are grounds for setting aside an election. These also may be an unfair labor practice. But statements that are not sufficiently coercive to constitute an unfair labor practice still may be the basis for setting an election aside when considered in the light of the "economic realities" of the employer-employee relationship. (53 LRRM 1019)

► A union's promise to employees that an initiation fee would be waived if the union won the election has been a matter of controversy among the Board and the courts. One view has been that such a promise warrants setting the election aside. A second view has been that such a promise warrants setting the election aside *only* if it is conditioned upon the union's winning the election. Another view has been that the waiver is valid provided no strings are attached, such as how the election turns out or how the employees vote. (58 LRRM 2419, 40 LRRM 116, 64 LRRM 1476, 74 LRRM 2664)

The Supreme Court resolved the issue in 1974 when it held that a union interfered with an election when it offered to waive initiation fees for all employees who signed union "recognition slips" before the election. But, the Court added, such a waiver is valid if it applies to employees who join the union after the election as well as those who join before. (84 LRRM 2929)

COUNTING THE BALLOTS

Each party to an election may appoint observers to act as checkers at the polls, assist in the counting of ballots, assist in the identification of voters, challenge voters, and otherwise assist the Board agent. Unless the parties agree otherwise, the observers must be nonsupervisory employees.

The counting of the ballots, however, may be observed by other persons designated by the parties, including supervisors and executives. Unless there is agreement among all the observers, the

Board agent makes the determination as to the validity of a ballot. Any party may press its disagreement with the determination by filing timely objections.

CERTIFICATION OF UNION

If no objections to the election are filed or if those that are filed are rejected, the Board then will issue a certification. There are two main types of certification: (1) a certification of representative, which is issued after an election in which a majority of the employees voted for a union; and (2) a certificate of the results of the election, which is issued after an election in which a majority of the employees failed to vote for union representation.

There are a number of benefits that accrue to the union—and some to the employer—from a certification. For example:

▶ The employer must bargain with the certified union for at least one year. (35 LRRM 2158)

▶ A certified union may strike to force the employer to assign work to members of the union in accordance with the certification. This is discussed in more detail in the chapter on "Strikes, Picketing, Boycotts, and Lockouts."

▶ A rival union may not engage in a strike in a strike or picketing for recognition in the face of the certification. This also is discussed in more detail in the later chapter.

▶ Even if the parties do not sign a collective bargaining contract, a rival union normally will not be able to petition for an election within a year of the certification.

▶ If a contract is signed within a year of the certification, it usually will bar a rival union's petition for the contract's duration up to a maximum of three years under the so-called contract-bar rules.

▶ Under its Bekins Motor rule, the Board will conduct an election, even though a union is alleged to discriminate on an invidious (racial) basis. But it will not certify the the union if the allegations of invidious discrimination are established. (86 LRRM 1323)

See below under "The Duty to Bargain" for a further discussion of this issue.

CONTRACT-BAR RULES

One of the prime purposes of the Taft-Hartley Act is to promote stable employer-union relationships under contracts covering terms and conditions of employment. In pursuit of this objective, the NLRB has established the contract-bar doctrine. In brief, the doctrine is that a current and valid contract between an employer and a union ordinarily will bar an election sought by a rival union.

The doctrine is not mentioned in the Act itself or in any regulations of the Board. It has been laid down in a long line of decisions by the Board. These decisions have woven a complex pattern of rules—rules that establish when a contract will operate as an election bar and when a rival union's election petition will be recognized and processed. Here are some of the main points:

▶ A union-security contract that is "clearly unlawful on its face" or that has been found unlawful in an unfair labor practice proceeding will not bar an election. But a contract may bar an election even though it contains a hot-cargo clause that is unlawful under the Act. (51 LRRM 1444, 49 LRRM 1774)

▶ Any contract of definite duration with a term of up to three years will bar an election for its entire term. A contract lasting longer than three years will bar an election sought by an outside union only for its first three years, but it will bar an election sought by the company or contracting union (if certified) for its full term. (50 LRRM 1137, 51 LRRM 1444)

▶ Contracts having no fixed duration are not considered an election bar for any period. (42 LRRM 1477)

▶ A petition filed during the term of an existing contract will be considered timely and will be processed only if it is filed more than 60 days but not more than 90 days before the termination date of the contract. (49 LRRM 1901)

▶ A contract that is prematurely extended will not bar an election if the petition is filed over 60 but not more than 90 days before the expiration date of the original contract. (42 LRRM 1475)

▶ Notice to modify or actual modification of a contract during its term won't remove the contract as a bar to an election. (42 LRRM 1470)

▶ A petition filed by a rival union during the 60-day period preceding the expiration of a contract will not be entertained by the Board even though the contract contains an automatic-renewal clause. A petition filed after the expiration date of an automatic-renewal contract will be accepted only if (1) employer and the incumbent union have failed to execute a new contract during the 60-day period; (2) automatic renewal was forestalled by timely notice of one of the parties; and (3) the rival union's petition was filed prior to the execution of a new contract. (42 LRRM 1470)

▶ A schism within a union will remove a contract as a bar to an election where (1) there is a basic intra-union conflict; (2) this conflict has resulted in such action by the employees that stability can be restored only by an election; (3) there has been an open meeting, with due notice, for the purpose of considering disaffiliation; (4) a disaffiliation vote was taken within a reasonable period after the conflict arose; and (5) the employer is faced with conflicting representation claims. A "basic intra-union conflict" was found by the Board to exist both in the cases of the unions expelled from the CIO on charges of Communism and those expelled from the AFL-CIO on charges of corruption. (34 LRRM 1023, 42 LRRM 1022, 42 LRRM 1461)

DECERTIFICATION ELECTIONS

A union may lose, as well as win, a certification as bargaining representative in the NLRB-conducted election. A petition for an election to decertify a union may be filed by a union, an employee, or a group of employees. But such a petition may not be filed by either an employer or a supervisor.

There is a 30-percent requirement for decertification, as well as representation, elections. The Board will direct a decertification election only if 30 percent of the employees in the unit support the petition. The contract-bar and other Board election rules apply to decertification elections in the same way that they apply to representation elections. But the only appropriate unit for a decertification election is the unit covered by the certification. The Board, for example, will not entertain a decertification petition by a group of craftsmen who are part of a plant-wide production and maintenance unit. (35 LRRM 1453)

CARD-CHECK BARGAINING ORDERS

For 10 years prior to May 1964, a union that proceeded to an election was precluded from filing an unfair labor practice charge based on the employer's refusal to recognize and bargain with the union prior to the election. But on May 4, 1964, the NLRB announced the Bernel Foam doctrine under which a union that proceeds to an election and loses it thereafter may file an unfair practice charge alleging that the employer unlawfully refused to recognize and bargain with it prior to the election—and the NLRB now will act on the charge.

The authority of the NLRB to issue a bargaining order on the basis of authorization cards in certain circumstances was upheld by the Supreme Court in the Gissel Packing case. A bargaining order is an appropriate and authorized remedy, the Court ruled, where an employer rejects a card majority while at the same time committing unfair labor practices that tend to undermine the union's majority and make a fair election an unlikely possibility. So far as the cards are concerned, the Court ruled that employees should be bound by the clear language of what they sign unless that language deliberately and clearly is canceled by a union adherent with words calculated to direct the signer to disregard the language above his signature. (71 LRRM 2481)

Following the Supreme Court's decision, the NLRB restated its position as follows: (1) A bargaining order may be issued to redress unfair labor practices so coercive that such an order would be needed to repair their unlawful effects even in the absence of a bargaining violation; and (2) where the unlawful conduct is less flagrant, the Board may find a bargaining violation and issue a bargaining order if the possibility of erasing the effect of the unfair practices and ensuring a fair election by the use of traditional remedies is slight and the employees' preference, as expressed through authorization cards, would be protected better by a bargaining order. (72 LRRM 103, 72 LRRM 1112) But see above under "Questioning of Employees" for a Board decision issuing a bargaining order where the employer questioned all employees in the unit and found that the union represented a majority. (81 LRRM 1313)

THE DUTY TO BARGAIN

The duty to bargain under the Taft-Hartley Act is two-edged. An employer is obligated to bargain in good faith with a union representing a majority of the employees in an appropriate unit. And a majority union is obligated to bargain in good faith with the employer. But neither is required "to agree to a proposal" made by the other or to make "a concession."

SUBJECTS FOR BARGAINING

The Act specifies that an employer and a majority union must bargain in good faith concerning wages, hours, and other terms and conditions of employment. Going on from there, the NLRB—with the approval of the U.S. Supreme Court—has recognized three categories of bargaining proposals and has established three sets of rules for them. They are:

Illegal Subjects—These are the demands that would be illegal and forbidden under the Act, such as a proposal for a closed shop. Bargaining on these subjects may not be required, and they may not be included in the contract even if the other party agrees.

Voluntary Subjects—These are the topics that fall outside the mandatory category of "wages, hours, and other conditions of employment." They may be placed on the bargaining table for voluntary bargaining and agreement. The other party, however, may not be required either to bargain on them or to agree to their inclusion in a contract. Insistence on them as a condition to the execution of a contract will be a violation of the bargaining duty.

Mandatory Subjects—These are the subjects that fall within the category of "wages, hours, and other terms and conditions of employment." Both the employer and the union are required to bargain in good faith with respect to them. (42 LRRM 2034)

MANDATORY BARGAINING SUBJECTS

The category of mandatory subjects of bargaining has been given specific meaning by a long line of NLRB and court decisions.

Included in the category, for example, are such topics as:

▶ Discharge of employees. (6 LRRM 674)

▶ Seniority, grievances, and working schedules. (22 LRRM 2506, 28 LRRM 1015, 30 LRRM 2602)

▶ Union security and checkoff. (24 LRRM 2561, 32 LRRM 2225)

▶ Vacations and individual merit raises. (31 LRRM 1072, 21 LRRM 2238)

▶ Retirement and pension and group insurance plans. (22 LRRM 2506, 24 LRRM 2068)

▶ Christmas bonuses and profit-sharing retirement plan. (31 LRRM 2057, 33 LRRM 2567)

▶ Employee stock purchase plan providing for employer contributions and making benefits partly dependent on length of service. (37 LRRM 2327)

▶ A non-discriminatory union hiring hall. (53 LRRM 1299)

▶ Plant rules on rest or lunch periods. (21 LRRM 1095)

▶ Safety rules, even though the employer may be under legal obligation to provide safe and healthful conditions of employment. (66 LRRM 2501)

▶ Company-owned houses occupied by the employees, as well as the rent paid for the houses. (28 LRRM 2434, 70 LRRM 2409)

▶ No-strike clauses binding on all employees in the bargaining unit. (22 LRRM 1158, 43 LRRM 1507)

▶ A nondiscriminatory hiring hall. (59 LRRM 3013)

▶ Physical examinations employees are required to take. (56 LRRM 1369)

▶ Insurance plans, even though the employer proposed to improve the insurance programs and the expiring agreement contained no provisions concerning the plans. (80 LRRM 1240)

▶ The privilege of exclusive hunting on a reserved portion of the company's forest preserve, a privilege that had existed for 20 years before the company proposed to discontinue it. (63 LRRM 1386)

▶ A "bar list" maintained by an oil company of former employees and others who were barred from entering the company's refineries. (66 LRRM 1038)

The NLRB held in the Fibreboard Paper case that the employer had to bargain about an economic decision to subcontract bargaining-unit work. It later applied the same rule to economic decisions to automate and to close a plant resulting in elimination of bargaining-unit work. The Supreme Court upheld the NLRB's Fibreboard decision but limited its holding to "the facts of the case" and said that the ruling did not encompass other forms of subcontracting. The Court emphasized that the Fibreboard subcontract did not alter the company's basic operation, but merely replaced existing employees with those of a contractor to do the same work under similar conditions (57 LRRM 2609). The NLRB later set out a series of tests for lawful unilateral subcontracting, including whether the subcontracting followed established practice and had no demonstrable adverse effect on employees in the unit. (58 LRRM 1257)

After the Fibreboard decision, the Third and the Eighth Circuit Courts of Appeals held that an employer is not required to bargain about major decisions involving a change in the nature of the company's business, a change in the capital structure, or moving or consolidating a failing business. But they did hold that an employer must bargain with the union about the effects of such decisions on the employees. (60 LRRM 2084, 60 LRRM 2033)

In a decision handed down in 1966, the NLRB refused to accept the rationale of these court opinions. (63 LRRM 1264) But in 1972, after the composition of the Board had changed, the Board accepted the principles laid down by the Third and Eighth Circuits and held that an employer did not have to bargain with the union about such major decisions affecting the nature of his business, but he did have to bargain about the effects of the change on his business. (79 LRRM 1396)

In two cases handed down prior to Fibreboard, the Board relied on contract clauses in holding that employers were not obligated to bargain about subcontracting—one limiting subcontracting to contractors paying wages comparable to those paid in the bargaining unit, the other a management rights clause giving the company the unrestricted right "to alter, rearrange, change, limit, or curtail its operations or any part thereof." (57 LRRM 1271, 1275; 57 LRRM 1217)

A post-Fibreboard decision cleared a company of a charge of violating the Act by failing to bargain with the union about a decision to make a partial plant closure. The decision, the NLRB pointed out, involved a major change in the nature of the business by discontinuing the manufacture of a product utilizing the skills of the employees who worked in the discontinued operation. (79 LRRM 1396)

One of the most controversial issues relating to mandatory bargaining subjects involves benefits for retired employees. The NLRB held that retirees remain "employees" under the Act and that, accordingly, the employer must bargain about increases in retirees' benefits. But the U.S. Court of Appeals for the Sixth Circuit reversed the holding. The Supreme Court upheld the Sixth Circuit finding that retirees are not "employees" under the Act. (71 LRRM 1433, 74 LRRM 2425, 78 LRRM 2974)

Even though companies are not required to bargain about benefits of retirees, many do so on a voluntary basis. These include such major industries as auto manufacturing and basic steel, which included a cost-of-living escalator clause for retirees in its 1974 contract.

VOLUNTARY BARGAINING SUBJECTS

There has not been as much delineation of voluntary subjects of bargaining—those that may be advanced but not insisted upon as a condition to an agreement. The following, however, have been placed in this category: (1) a clause making the local union the exclusive bargaining agent, even though the international union was the certified agent (42 LRRM 2034); (2) a clause requiring a secret-ballot vote among the employees on the employer's last offer before a strike could be called (42 LRRM 2034); (3) a clause fixing the size and membership of the employer or union bargaining teams (31 LRRM 2422); (4) a requirement that a contract must be ratified by a secret employee ballot (38 LRRM 2574), though the method of ratification is an internal union concern (73 LRRM 2097); (5) a clause providing that a contract will become void whenever more than 50 percent of the employees fail to authorize dues checkoff (38 LRRM 2574); (6) a requirement that the union post a performance bond or an indemnity bond to compensate the employer for losses caused by picketing by other unions (32 LRRM 3684, 49 LRRM 1831); (7) a requirement that employers post a cash bond to cover any assessment for wages or fringe payments due under the contract, or guarantee to pay to the union a sum equivalent to the initiation fees the union would have received for each employee not included in the bargaining unit if the employer violated a clause barring subcontracting to employers not parties to the master contract (66 LRRM 2333, 69 LRRM 2944); (8) a clause fixing terms and conditions of employment for workers hired to replace strikers (19 LRRM 1199); (9) strike insurance obtained by employers to guard against the financial risks involved in a strike (76 LRRM 1033); (10) the price of meals furnished or sold to employees in a cafeteria operated by an independent caterer (66 LRRM 2634, 75 LRRM 2223); and (11) benefits of retirees. (78 LRRM 2974)

AUTHORITY, SELECTION OF NEGOTIATORS

There is no general rule on how much authority an employer or a union must vest in its negotiator in order to meet the good-faith bargaining obligation. The question has been handled by the NLRB and the courts on a case-by-case basis.

One court has held, however, that nothing in the Act requires a party to give complete authority to reach an agreement to a negotiator. Failure to vest authority in a negotiator isn't of itself evidence of bad-faith bargaining, the court said. But the degree of authority given to the negotiator may be considered in determining whether there was good-faith bargaining. (35 LRRM 2009)

One of the 1947 Taft-Hartley amendments to the Act made it an unfair labor practice for a union to restrain or coerce an employer in the selection of his bargaining representative. Applying this provision, the Board has held that a union violated the Act by refusing to meet with an attorney who had been selected to represent the employer in negotiating a new contract. (47 LRRM 2089)

But a union was cleared of violation charges in another case in which the union refused to bargain with a management negotiator who previously had held a highly confidential position in the union. A court said that the employer had displayed an absence of fair dealing in insisting that the former union official represent him in negotiations. (45 LRRM 2626)

Although there is no specific statutory prohibition against employer attempts to dictate the choice of union bargaining representatives, the NLRB has held that attempts by an employer to limit the size or composition of a union's bargaining committee are a violation of the good-faith bargaining duty (28 LRRM 1559, 30 LRRM 2479, 37 LRRM 1030). This includes a refusal to meet with a union's negotiating committee because of the presence of representatives of other unions. This is the "coalition" or "coordinated" bargaining technique. The NLRB decision was upheld by the U.S. Court of Appeals for the Second Circuit, although the court agreed with dissenting NLRB Member Zagoria that the company did not violate the Act by refusing to meet with the "coordinated" or "coalition" team for preliminary discussions prior to the formal reopening of the basic contract between the Electrical Workers (IUE) and General Electric Co. A similar holding on coordinated bargaining was handed down by the U.S. Court of Appeals for the Eighth Circuit in a case involving the Minnesota Mining and Manufacturing Co. and the Oil, Chemical and Atomic Workers. (71 LRRM 2418, 72 LRRM 2129)

In another case, however, the NLRB held that a union unlawfully tried to force an employer to engage in company-wide bargaining, thus seeking unilaterally to change the bargaining unit, by insisting on simultaneous and satisfactory settlement of contracts in other bargaining units of the company and striking in support of such demands. The decision of the NLRB, however, was reversed by the U.S. Court of Appeals for the Third Circuit. The case was denied review by the U.S. Supreme Court. (81 LRRM 2893)

On the other hand, an employer was held to have violated the Act by insisting to the point of impasse on joint negotiations with unions representing different units of the company's employees. The Board said the company was infringing upon a basic employee right—the right of employees to select their own bargaining representative. (72 LRRM 1465)

CONDUCT OF NEGOTIATIONS

The duty to bargain in good faith is defined in the Taft-Hartley Act as requiring the representatives of the employer and the union "to meet at reasonable times and confer in good faith with respect to wages, hours, and other terms and conditions of employment." It also requires the execution of a written contract incorporating any agreement reached if requested by either party. But it does not require either party to agree to a proposal or to make a concession.

Applying these tests, the NLRB and the courts have made it clear that merely going through the motions of bargaining isn't sufficient. The NLRB based a violation finding in one leading case on a company's over-all approach to and conduct of bargaining. (57 LRRM 1491) The test is whether the party's attitude, on the entire record, indicates a good-faith desire to reach an agreement with the other party. But this doesn't require "fruitless marathon discussions at the expense of frank statement and support of one's position." (30 LRRM 2147)

In the leading H. K. Porter case, the Supreme Court held that the NLRB has no authority to compel an employer or a union to agree to any substantive provision of a collective bargaining contract. Specifically, the Court held that the Board had no authority to order a company to agree to a dues check-off, even though the court upheld the Board's finding that the company had not bargained in good faith. (73 LRRM 2561)

One of the most difficult problems the Board has faced in fashioning remedies in refusal-to-bargain cases is whether it has authority to issue "make-whole" orders. A "make-whole" order requires the employer to reimburse the employees retroactively for the increased wages and fringe benefits the employer would have agreed to if he had bargained in good faith. The NLRB decided by a three-to-two vote that it did not have authority to issue such an order. (74 LRRM 1740)

But the U.S. Court of Appeals for the District of Columbia ruled that the Board has ample authority under the Act to issue a "make-whole" order to provide meaningful relief for employees unlawfully denied the fruits of collective bargaining. It handed down the ruling in a case in which it found that the employer's reasons for challenging the union's certification were "patently frivolous." (73 LRRM 2870)

On remand of the case from the court, the NLRB still refused to issue a "make-whole" order even though it found that the employer had committed a "clear and flagrant" violation of the law. But it did require the company to reimburse the Board and the union for their respective expenses incurred in investigation, preparation, and conduct of the cases both at the Board and court levels. It also required the company to furnish the union with the names and addresses of employees in the bargaining unit and to give the union access to company bulletin boards. (79 LRRM 1175, 79 LRRM 1693)

EMPLOYER BARGAINING

The cases charging bad-faith bargaining by employers have been much more numerous than those charging similar conduct by unions. Lack of good faith on the part of an employer may be indicated by such conduct as:

▶ A refusal to discuss or consider the proposals of the union. (22 LRRM 1359)

▶ Use of delaying tactics, frequent postponements of bargaining sessions. (24 LRRM 1653)

▶ Withdrawal of concessions previously granted. (20 LRRM 1203)

▶ Insisting that the union provide a performance bond before any contract will be executed with it. (32 LRRM 2684)

▶ Negotiating directly with individual employees after the bargaining agent had requested negotiations or while such negotiations were pending (14 LRRM 581)

▶ Unilateral action on matters that are properly the subject of bargaining, such as changing plant rules or production quotas or announcing new piece rates. According to the U.S. Supreme Court, such unilateral action may *of itself* be a violation. (50 LRRM 2177)

▶ Refusing to furnish the union with data needed by it to bargain intelligently. (10 LRRM 49) (The type of data that must be furnished is discussed in more detail below.)

▶ Over-all conduct both at and away from the bargaining table. (This is the well-known General Electric decision.) (57 LRRM 1491, 72 LRRM 2530) The Board adhered to its decision in the General Electric case in holding that U.S. Gypsum Company violated the Act by engaging in mere "surface" bargaining that included many of the practices in the 1960 General Electric negotiations. (82 LRRM 1064)

Prior to this decision, however, the Board cleared an employer of charges of violating the bargaining duty, even though the bargaining covered 28 months and 74 formal negotiating sessions, and the employer communicated extensively with the employees during the negotiations. The Board pointed to the company's willingness to make concessions and to its "fair and factual" communications with the employees. (62 LRRM 1617)

Lawful Tactics and Conduct—Examining each case on the basis of its own particular facts, the NLRB and the courts also have found a variety of tactics and conduct as not indicating a lack of good faith in bargaining. Some examples are: (1) insisting on absolute "uniformity" of wage and other money items for the company's unionized and nonunionized employees (33 LRRM 2883); (2) refusing to offer a counterproposal in the face of an uncompromising position of the union (28 LRRM 1539); (3) giving little and holding fast to many of the company's initial positions (46 LRRM 1390); (4) refusing to offer a second counterproposal (29 LRRM 2206); (5) insisting on a no-strike clause without an arbitration clause and on limiting the grievance committee to employees (46 LRRM 2374); and (6) substantially adhering to a "final offer" in seven negotiating sessions (52 LRRM 1184).

UNION BARGAINING

There have been comparatively few Board and court decisions on what union conduct amounts to a refusal to bargain in good faith. In a landmark decision handed down in 1961, however, the U.S. Supreme Court ruled that a union's resort to unprotected harassing tactics (refusing to write new business during certain periods, to make reports as specified, to participate in conferences, etc.) as a means of putting pressure on the employer during bargaining did not amount to a violation of the bargaining duty. While an employer may have the right to discipline the union members for such tactics, the Court said, this does not make the tactics an unfair labor practice. (45 LRRM 2704)

A union's insistence that the employer post a performance bond as a condition to the settlement of a strike, however, has been held to be a violation of the bargaining duty (29 LRRM 2617). The same is true of a union's insistence that any agreement that might be reached contain a hiring-hall provision outlawed by the Act (24 LRRM 2268). And a union that insisted that the bargaining unit include employees found to be supervisors also was held to have violated its bargaining duty (30 LRRM 1288).

Duty of Fair Representation — It has been held both under the Railway Labor Act and the Taft-Hartley Act that a union must represent all members of the bargaining unit without invidious discrimination. But the Supreme Court has ruled that a breach of the duty of fair representation occurs only when a union's conduct with respect to a member of the bargaining unit is arbitrary, discriminatory, or in bad faith. (64 LRRM 2369)

The remedial machinery under the Act is not available to a union that practices racial discrimination. On this basis the Eighth Circuit Court of Appeals remanded a case to the NLRB to determine whether this is a relevant area of inquiry when raised by an employer in defense of a refusal to bargain with the union. (82 LRRM 2608) The Board accepted the court's reasoning in the Bekins Moving case. It decided that it would conduct an election in the face of allegations of invidious discrimination by the union. But if the union won the election, the employer could then press objections based on the alleged discrimination. If they were established, the union would not be certified as bargaining representative. (86 LRRM 1323)

DATA FOR BARGAINING

To meet his bargaining duty under the Act, an employer is required to furnish a union bargaining agent, on request, with sufficient data on wage rates, job classifications, and allied matters to permit the union (1) to bargain understandingly, (2) to police the administration of the current contract, and (3) to prepare for coming negotiations. Such information must be provided even though the employer considers it confidential. (11 LRRM 693, 35 LRRM 2709, 25 LRRM 1475)

The information an employer is required to furnish the union may cover a broad range of topics. Employers have been required, for example, to furnish the following, although it need not be in the exact form the union requests: (1) arbitration claim files necessary to evaluate the employer's compliance with an award (67 LRRM 1553); (2) information relating to the cost of proposed improvements in existing welfare programs (61 LRRM 2657); (3) wage and fringe benefit information for 16 classifications outside the bargaining unit (81 LRRM 1420); information relating to the exact salaries paid employees in the unit, including salaries in excess of those specified in the union contract (69 LRRM 1100); time-study and job evaluation data (41 LRRM 2679); dates of employment and seniority standing of individual employees (36 LRRM 2576); number of hours worked by individual employees (34 LRRM 1319); job classifications, job descriptions, wage rates, and rate ranges (32 LRRM 2709); production standards used in determining merit ratings (26 LRRM 1333); changes in productivity in the plant (30 LRRM 1265); pension and group insurance data (32 LRRM 2225); and time studies and the employer's method of making them. (31 LRRM 1334)

On the question of time studies, the NLRB held in 1964 that a company was obligated to let a union make its own time studies of disputed operations. It found that the time studies were relevant and necessary to the union's administration of the grievance machinery of the contract and that the needed information was not available to the union through alternative channels (56 LRRM 1108). The decision was upheld by the U.S. Court of Appeals at New York (62 LRRM 2415).

Where geography and other circumstances make it extremely difficult for a union bargaining representative to communicate with members of the bargaining unit, the employer may be required to furnish the union with a list of the names and addresses of all employees in the unit represented by the union. (69 LRRM 2014, 71 LRRM 2254, 75 LRRM 2692)

Wage Data Obtained in Confidence — In a 1970 case, the NLRB held that a company that conducted an area wage survey violated the Act when it refused to furnish an incumbent union with correlated data tying job classifications and pay rates to the specific companies surveyed. The union challenged the data, but the company refused to reveal the companies from which the rates had been obtained, stating that they had been obtained in confidence. The Board rejected the company's position, stating that information is not exempt from disclosure merely because it was obtained in confidence. (74 LRRM 1444)

In a 1972 decision, the U.S. Court of Appeals at Cincinnati held that General Electric Co. violated the Act by refusing to disclose data obtained by wage surveys in four locations. The company was using the data in bargaining as a basis for refusing to raise wages at the plants. (81 LRRM 2303)

Data on Company's Financial Condition — If an employer pleads inability to meet a union's financial demands during negotiations, he also may be required to supply the union with financial data to back up his plea. But this obligation does not "automatically" follow a claim of inability to pay. It depends on the facts and circumstances of each case. Nor is the employer required to substantiate the claim; it is enough if he attempts to substantiate it (38 LRRM 2042, 47 LRRM 1472). The same duty to provide substantiating data attaches to an employer who claims that competitive disadvantage precludes him from granting a wage increase (61 LRRM 2218).

Data That Need Not Be Furnished — Certain data, however, need not be furnished the union. They include, for example, the following: point information used in evaluating the various elements of a job for classification purposes (57 LRRM 1001); information relating to the cost of a noncontributory group insurance program (48 LRRM 2313); cost information relating to the subcontracting of certain work, notwithstanding the union's contention that the information was needed to process grievances (69 LRRM 1251); a "competitive adder" to salary curves used to determine merit increases (76 LRRM 1637).

LIMITS ON UNION'S RIGHTS

Although an employer may be required to furnish the wage or financial data to a union, he can place some definite limitations on the manner and form in which it will be furnished. Some of these limitations are:

▶ An employer presumably may require the union to bear the additional cost of furnishing the requested data. (35 LRRM 2730)

▶ An employer is within his rights in refusing to permit a union to take job evaluation and job description records out of the plant for study and analysis. The same may be true with respect to information concerning customers and suppliers. (47 LRRM 1039, 47 LRRM 1472)

▶ An employer may refuse to supply detailed information as to past earnings of employees where compilation of the data would be unduly burdensome. (47 LRRM 1072)

▶ An employer may require that an audit of his books be done in his office and that any accountant the union appoints to do the audit be a licensed or certified public accountant. (47 LRRM 1472)

WITHDRAWAL FROM MULTI-EMPLOYER UNIT

The rules governing withdrawals from multi-employer units are the same for employers and unions. The withdrawal must be made before the date set for multi-employer negotiations, and the withdrawal must be unequivocal. The rules on employer withdrawals were established many years ago. They were applied to unions in 1966. (63 LRRM 2527)

SUCCESSOR EMPLOYERS

For a number of years, there was considerable controversy about the collective bargaining obligations of a company that acquired a business from another company having a contract or an established bargaining relationship with a union. In a landmark decision handed down in 1972, the Supreme Court laid down these rules:

▶ A successor employer who retains the employees of the predecessor employer is required to bargain with the union that represents a majority of the employees.

▶ But the successor employer is not required to honor the contract negotiated by the predecessor with the union. (80 LRRM 2225)

Subsequently, the Court held that an employer who acquires and operates in basically unchanged form the business of an employer found guilty of unfair labor practices under the Act under circumstances that charge the purchaser with notice of the unfair labor practice charges against the seller will be jointly and severally liable with the seller for remedying the unfair labor practices. (84 LRRM 2839)

A franchiser that purchased the assets of a restaurant and motor lodge and hired only a small fraction of the seller's employees was not required to arbitrate the extent of its obligations under the seller's collective bargaining contract to the seller's employees whom it did not hire. This was a Supreme Court decision. (86 LRRM 2449) The decision limits the scope of the John Wiley decision in which the Court held that the obligation to arbitrate disputes survived both the expiration of the contract and the disappearance of the corporate employer by merger. (55 LRRM 2769)

LAWFUL AND UNLAWFUL
UNION SECURITY CLAUSES

Although the Supreme Court has told the NLRB that it should not sit in judgment on particular clauses to be included in collective bargaining agreements, there are certain clauses that may not be included in a contract. These clauses relate to compulsory union membership or, in union parlance, union security.

There are a number of types of union security clauses. The following are the principal ones:

Closed Shop — These clauses require that the employer hire only members of a particular union.

Full Union Shop — Under these clauses an employer may hire an employee who is not a member of the union but all employees must join the union within a specified period of time, usually 30 days after hiring.

Modified Union Shop — The most common form of modified union shop requires new employees to join the union and present employees and all who join to maintain their union membership. However, old employees who are not members of the union may continue to stay out of the union.

Maintenance of Membership — These clauses require persons who become union members to continue their membership, but they do not impose any membership requirement on other employees.

Agency Shop — These clauses obligate employees who do not join the union to pay the equivalent of union dues and fees for the union's services. The money so paid sometimes goes to the union welfare fund, instead of to the union treasury.

Hiring Arrangements — There is a wide variety of such arrangements, but their general purpose is to favor or protect union members in obtaining jobs.

TAFT-HARTLEY RESTRICTIONS

Under the Taft-Hartley Act, it is an unfair labor practice for an employer to discriminate against an employee or applicant for employment either because he is a member of a union or because he is not a member of a union. It also is an unfair labor practice for a union to cause an employer so to discriminate.

A proviso to Section 8 (a) (3), however, permits an employer and a union to agree to a limited form of union shop. If a union is the majority bargaining agent, it may sign a union-shop contract subject to the following conditions:

▶ Membership may be required only after 30 days following the effective date of the contract or the beginning of employment, whichever is later.

▶ The union must admit eligible employees to membership without discrimination, although the union retains the right to make its own rules of eligibility.

▶ When a union-shop contract has been made under these conditions, the union may seek an employee's discharge for non-membership only when membership has been withdrawn for failure to tender an initiation fee or the periodic dues.

Exceptions for Construction Industry — The 1959 amendments to the Act, however, established some special union security rules for the building and construction industry. These rules permit a building trades employer to make a pre-hire, union-shop contract with a construction union under these conditions:

▶ The contract may be executed before the majority status of the union has been established under the Act.

▶ The contract may require employees to join the union seven days after their employment or after the effective date of the contract, whichever is later.

▶ The contract may require the employer to notify the union of job opportunities and to give the union an opportunity to refer qualified applicants.

▶ The agreement may specify minimum training or experience qualifications for employment or provide for priority in opportunities for employment based upon length of service with the employer, in the industry, or in the geographical area.

UNION HIRING-HALL RULES

The use of union hiring halls as employment agencies has been a common practice in industries in which employment is casual or intermittent, such as the construction and longshoring industries. Up until 1958, the NLRB judged the legality of such hiring arrangements on a case-by-case basis. But in its 1958 Mountain

Pacific decision, the Board held that an exclusive union hiring hall would be legal only if it met these standards:

▶ Union referrals are made on a nondiscriminatory basis without regard to union membership or lack of union membership.

▶ The employer retains the right to reject any applicant referred by the union.

▶ All provisions relating to the hiring arrangement are posted where notices to employees and applicants for employment customarily are posted. (41 LRRM 1460)

The Supreme Court, however, reversed a decision applying this rule. It upheld a hiring-hall agreement that specifically stated that there would be no discrimination. There was no evidence of actual discrimination. The Court did not rule out the possibility of considering lack of the standards as evidence of discrimination. (47 LRRM 2906)

Brown-Olds Penalty — As a penalty for violation of these standards, the Board has required the parties to an unlawful hiring-hall arrangement to refund to employees all initiation fees and dues collected under the agreement during the six months preceding the filing of an unfair labor practice charge. This is known as the Brown-Olds penalty, it having been first invoked in a case bearing that name (37 LRRM 1360). The Supreme Court, however, reversed a decision applying the penalty. It said that a dues-refund order is punitive and invalid in the absence of evidence that any individual was coerced to join or remain in the union (47 LRRM 2900).

Maintenance of Membership — Maintenance-of-membership clauses are regarded as a lesser form of union security than the union shop. The NLRB has held that such clauses are valid under the Taft-Hartley Act. (29 LRRM 1224)

But the Board also has held that maintenance-of-membership clauses are subject to all the limitations that apply to the union shop. Thus employees who lose their membership in a union may be discharged pursuant to the agreement only if they were expelled for nonpayment of dues or initiation fees. (29 LRRM 1295)

UNION-SHOP DEAUTHORIZATION ELECTIONS

Suppose employees in a unit covered by a valid union-shop contract decide they no longer want a union shop. The NLRB will conduct a union-shop deauthorization election. A petition for such an election may be filed by 30 percent of the employees in the unit or by an employee or group acting on behalf of them. The usual contract-bar rules do not apply to such petitions, although the unit must be the same as that covered by the contract. If a majority of the employees *eligible to vote,* not merely those who cast ballots, vote for deauthorization, the union-shop clause is suspended.

STATE RIGHT-TO-WORK LAWS

Under Section 14 (b) of the Taft-Hartley Act, there is a specific sanction for state laws that regulate union security more strictly than does the federal act. In line with this sanction, 20 states have so-called right-to-work laws aimed at outlawing most, if not all, forms of union security. These 20 states are: Alabama, Arizona, Arkansas, Florida, Georgia, Iowa, Kansas, Louisiana (limited to agricultural workers), Mississippi, Nebraska, Nevada, North Carolina, North Dakota, South Carolina, South Dakota, Tennessee, Texas, Utah, Virginia, and Wyoming.

The constitutionality of these laws was upheld by the U.S. Supreme Court in 1949 (23 LRRM 2199, 2204). The agency shop, under which nonmembers have to pay the equivalent of union dues, has been held unlawful under the right-to-work laws of most of the states. In three decisions handed down in 1963, the Supreme Court held that an agency shop is lawful under the Taft-Hartley Act, but added that the states have the authority to outlaw agency-shop contracts under the sanction provided by Section 14 (b) of the Taft-Hartley Act. A state thus may declare such a contract illegal and enjoin its enforcement. (53 LRRM 2313, 53 LRRM 2318, 54 LRRM 2612)

In describing the effect of Section 14 (b), the Supreme Court said that Congress left the states free to legislate in the field of union security agreements, and it did not deprive them of the power to enforce their laws restricting the execution and enforcement of such agreements. But the state power recognized in Section 14 (b) begins only with the actual negotiation and enforcement of the union security agreement. So picketing to obtain union security agreements remains within the exclusive jurisdiction of the NLRB, while the states have the power to declare a contract illegal and enjoin its enforcement, including ordering reinstatement with back pay of an employee discharged under a contract that violates the state law. (54 LRRM 2612)

In a case placing a limitation on right-to-work laws, an appeals court held that a hiring-hall arrangement expressly stating that union membership is not to be considered in job referrals is not subject to state regulation under a right-to-work law. Although Section 14

(b) permits right-to-work laws, it does not protect a state law that is so broadly stated or construed as to bar such nondiscriminatory hiring-hall arrangements. (60 LRRM 2434)

STRIKES, PICKETING, BOYCOTTS, AND LOCKOUTS

In the background of every labor controversy is the possibility of a strike by the employees or a lockout by the employer. These are the ultimate weapons of industrial strife when negotiations break down.

The concerted stoppage of work known as a strike, however, may be of little effect in enforcing the workers' demands if the employer is able to replace the strikers and resume normal production. To prevent such an outcome, unions customarily resort to picketing. They also may resort to picketing as a means of exerting pressure on an employer from whom they are seeking recognition as a bargaining agent.

In its simplest form, picketing is merely a type of advertising. It informs the public — and other workers — that there is a strike or dispute and states the union's version of its cause. But if feelings run high, the picketing may take the form of persuading customers not to patronize the employer or other employees not to enter the employer's premises.

Closely tied in with strikes and picketing is the boycott. A simple or primary boycott is a refusal to deal with, patronize, or permit union members to work for an employer with whom the union has a dispute. At times, however, it is found by the union to be more effective to act against the customers or suppliers of the target employer. The boycott then becomes a secondary boycott. The union may set up a picket line at the premises of the customers or suppliers — the neutral or secondary employers.

THE LABOR INJUNCTION

For many years, the usual response of an employer to picketing and boycotts was to go into court and obtain an injunction against the union. But in 1932, Congress adopted the Norris-LaGuardia Act forbidding the federal courts to issue injunctions in labor disputes unless certain prior conditions are fulfilled. A number of the states then adopted "Little Norris-LaGuardia Acts" patterned after the federal law.

Among the conditions that must be fulfilled before an injunction may be issued is that the union be given an opportunity to state its case; there may be no ex parte injunctions. A showing also must be made that all efforts to obtain a settlement by conciliation and other methods provided for by law have been exhausted and that the withholding of the injunction will cause more harm to one party than granting it will cause to the other party.

An exception to the law was made when the Supreme Court held that the Government might obtain an injunction against a strike directed at it as an employer operating an industrial property. An injunction issued against a strike of the coal mines at a time when they were being operated by the Government was upheld by the Court. (19 LRRM 2346)

The adoption in 1947 of the Taft-Hartley Act established a detailed federal code of law governing strikes, picketing, and boycotts. Additions were made to this code by the 1959 Landrum-Griffin amendments to the law.

TAFT-HARTLEY RESTRICTIONS

The Taft-Hartley Act specifically restricts the right to strike and to picket in several important respects. Section 8 (b) (4) makes it an unfair labor practice for a union or its agents to engage in or encourage a strike for any one of the following purposes:

▶ Forcing any employer or self-employed person to join a labor or employer organization or to enter into a hot-cargo contract. This is directed mainly against certain types of secondary boycotts.

▶ Forcing any person to cease doing business with any other person. This is the so-called secondary boycott.

▶ Forcing an employer other than the one employing the union's members to recognize as bargaining agent any union not certified by the NLRB. This is the so-called secondary-recognition strike.

▶ Forcing an employer to recognize a union as bargaining agent if another union already has been certified to represent his employees.

▶ Forcing an employer to transfer work from one group of employees to another group. This includes so-called work-jurisdiction or work-task picketing.

RECOGNITION PICKETING

Section 8 (b) (7) inserted in the Taft-Hartley Act by the 1959 amendments makes it unlawful for a union to picket "to force or require" the employer to recognize the union or the employees to accept it as bargaining agent where:

▶ Another union has been recognized as bargaining agent, and the NLRB would not conduct an election because a question of representation does not exist.

▶ A valid election has been conducted within the preceding 12 months.

▶ The picketing has been conducted for a reasonable period of time (not to exceed 30 days), and no election petition has been filed.

Sanctions Provided — Not only are strikes and picketing for the purposes mentioned above made unfair labor practices, but they also are subject to special sanctions. Except with respect to work task picketing, the NLRB's General Counsel is required to seek a federal court injunction against continuance of the strike or picketing if he believes that a formal unfair labor practice proceeding should be commenced by the issuance of a complaint. For work-task picketing and other types of unfair labor practices, the General Counsel has discretion with respect to seeking an injunction. The injunction ordinarily runs until the NLRB has issued a decision in the case.

In addition, any person injured by any of the enumerated types of strikes and picketing may sue for damages in the federal courts. This right is not granted by the Taft-Hartley Act with respect to other types of union conduct involving strikes and picketing, even though the conduct may involve unfair labor practices.

PUBLICIZING DISPUTE

Both the secondary-boycott prohibition and the provisions restricting recognition and organizational picketing contain provisos designed to preserve a union's right to publicize a dispute with an employer. The proviso in the secondary-boycott prohibition states that nothing in the provision should be construed to bar a union from using publicity for the purpose of "truthfully advising" the public, consumers, and union members that the neutral employer is distributing goods produced by an employer with whom the union has a dispute.

But two important conditions are attached to this right to publicize the dispute. They are:

▶ The union may not picket the neutral stores to persuade customers to stop trading with the stores in order to force the stores to stop dealing with the struck employer. But the union may picket the stores to persuade customers not to buy the products of the struck employer, who need not be a "manufacturer" of the products. This distinction was drawn by the Supreme Court. (55 LRRM 2961)

► The publicity must not induce employees of other employers to refuse to pick up, deliver, or transport any goods or to refuse to perform any services at the distributor's establishment. But it has been held by both the NLRB and one federal court of appeals that mere isolated interferences with pickups and deliveries will not remove the picketing from the protection of the publicity proviso. (51 LRRM 1053, 55 LRRM 2544)

The publicity proviso in the recognition picketing section is attached to the provision making it unlawful to picket for recognition or organizational purposes where no election petition is filed within a reasonable period of time. The proviso permits both picketing and other publicity for the purpose of truthfully advising the public of the dispute unless the effect is to stop deliveries or performance of services by employees of other employers.

Dual-Purpose Picketing — One of the first questions raised under the restrictions on recognition and organizational picketing was whether picketing that had a dual purpose — recognition and publicity — was prohibited. Reversing its initial interpretations of the provisions, the NLRB laid down these rules:

► Purely informational picketing is not barred under any of the three subsections of Section 8 (b) (7). To be subject to the ban, the picketing must have recognition or organization as an object. Thus, a union may engage in purely informational picketing without regard to whether another union has been lawfully recognized, a valid election has been conducted within the last 12 months, or no election petition was filed within a reasonable period of time.

► If picketing is purely informational, it is immaterial that it stops pickups or deliveries. This would not make it unlawful.

► Dual-purpose picketing — that which has both information and recognition as objects — comes within the protection of the proviso to Subsection (C). It becomes unlawful only if it stops pickups or deliveries. (49 LRRM 1648)

► *Moreover,* minor interference with pickups or deliveries will not make the picketing unlawful. The picketing will be unlawful only if it has "disrupted, interfered with, or curtailed the employer's business." (51 LRRM 1053, 55 LRRM 2544) However, picketing that is a "signal" to organized labor to stop work does not come within the protection of the proviso and is unlawful even though it does not stop deliveries or services. (52 LRRM 1508)

Although picketing to protect area labor standards does not come within the restriction on recognition picketing, picketing to compel an employer to sign a contract to pay wages and fringes equal to those paid under union contracts is recognition picketing subject to the Section 8 (b) (7) restrictions. (62 LRRM 2511) The NLRB previously had recognized picketing to protect area labor standards as being outside the recognition picketing restrictions. (49 LRRM 1757) But in later cases, the Board often was concerned with the truth of the union's assertion that the picketed employer paid substandard wages and fringes, since if the statement was not true, there could be a possible inference of some other object. (81 LRRM 1588)

The board earlier held that picketing to obtain the reinstatement of a discharged employee was not necessarily picketing to compel recognition or bargaining. (49 LRRM 1021)

SCOPE OF BOYCOTT BAN

Prior to the 1959 amendments to the Act, the scope of the secondary-boycott ban was quite limited. To establish a violation of the ban, it was necessary to show that the union induced or encouraged employees of a neutral employer to strike or refuse to perform services as a means of putting pressure on the neutral employer to stop doing business with a struck employer. There was nothing unlawful in a union's going directly to the neutral employer and by threats or other means getting him to stop doing business with the struck employer.

The 1959 amendments sought to close this loophole with new language. A somewhat broadened version of the old provision bars inducement or encouragement of individuals employed by neutral employers to strike or refuse to perform services. A new provision makes it unlawful for a union to use threats, coercion, or restraint to compel any "person" — a term that includes an employer — to stop doing business with another. Thus, it no longer is lawful for a union to effectuate a secondary boycott by putting pressure directly on a neutral employer or his managerial employees by threats, coercion or restraint to exercise their managerial discretion to stop doing business with the struck employer. (55 LRRM 2957)

A key Supreme Court decision held that if a union directs appeals to managerial employees of a neutral employer who does business with a struck employer, the appeals will violate the secondary-boycott provisions only if they are to induce the employees to withhold their services from their employer with an object of forcing him to stop doing business with the struck employer. If the appeals are to induce the employees to exercise their "managerial discretion" to stop doing business with the struck employer, they will violate the Act only if they threaten, coerce, or restrain the employees in the exercise of their managerial discretion. (55 LRRM 2957)

In addition to closing the loophole relating to threats, coercion, or restraint directed at the employer himself, the 1959 amendments made these additional changes:

▶ Unions were prohibited from inducing individual employees one at a time to engage in secondary boycotts.

▶ The boycott ban was extended to inducements of supervisors, farm labor, railroads, municipalities, and government agencies. The ban also applies to threats, coercion, or restraint of railroads, municipalities, or government agencies.

BOYCOTTS: PUBLICITY PROVISO

In an authorization for consumer appeals at retail stores, the 1959 amendments stated that nothing in the secondary boycott provisions shall be construed to prohibit a union from using publicity for the purpose of truthfully advising the public, consumers, and members of unions that goods are produced by an employer with whom the union has a dispute and are distributed by another employer. But two important conditions were attached:

▶ First, the union may not picket the neutral establishment.

▶ Second, the publicity may not induce employees of neutral employers to refuse to pick up, deliver, or transport any goods or to refuse to perform any services at the distributor's establishment.

The proviso, the Supreme Court ruled, is not limited to disputes in which the struck employer is a manufacturer. It applies, for example, to a wholesaler or distributor. (55 LRRM 2957) It also applies to a television station as the "producer" of the products advertised on its programs. (58 LRRM 1019)

Object of Picketing — Although the publicity proviso of the secondary-boycott provisions clearly forbids picketing of the retail stores, the Supreme Court ruled that it does not forbid *all* peaceful picketing of the stores. It only bars picketing to persuade customers to stop trading with the stores to force them to stop dealing with the struck employer. Picketing merely to persuade customers not to purchase the products of the struck employer is closely confined to the primary dispute and is not forbidden. (55 LRRM 2961)

In a later case, an appeals court said that while peaceful picketing to persuade customers to stop buying products of a struck or nonunion company is permissible, the product involved must be clearly identified and the picketing must not be aimed at inducing a general loss of business by the store. So a broad appeal "to look for the union label" is an unlawful secondary boycott. (67 LRRM 8392)

A union also was held to have violated the secondary-boycott ban by picketing a shopping center in an attempt to induce customers not to patronize four restaurants and one jewelry store that advertised in a newspaper with which the union had a dispute. The union's object was to force the restaurants and the store to stop advertising in the newspaper. Since the restaurants and the store advertised their entire businesses, not just their products, the picketing amounted to more than the mere following of a struck product. (68 LRRM 3004)

Common-Situs Picketing — Some of the most difficult cases under the secondary-boycott ban have been those involving picketing on a work site at which employees both of the struck employer and of neutral employers are working. The NLRB has established these tests for the legality of such common-situs picketing:

▶ Picketing must be limited to times when the struck employer's employees actually are present at the common site.

▶ Picketing must be limited to places "reasonably close" to the operations of the struck employer's workers.

▶ The pickets must show clearly that their dispute is with the struck employer alone.

▶ The struck employer's workers must be engaged in the employer's normal business. (27 LRRM 1108)

The NLRB has stressed, however, that these tests are not the sole guide for determining the legality of common-situs picketing. They are rather evidentiary in nature, and they are to be applied in the absence of more direct evidence of the intent and purpose of the union. The mere compliance with the four requirements does not immunize a union from charges of violation under the Act. (47 LRRM 2033, 81 LRRM 1461)

An appeals court ruled that an independently owned and operated warehouse in which a struck employer's products were stored was not a part of the struck employer's operation for the purpose of applying the rules on common-situs picketing. The mere presence of the struck employer's goods on the premises of a neutral employer under an established business relationship was not, of itself, sufficient to convert picketing of the neutral premises from unlawful secondary to lawful primary picketing. (75 LRRM 2752)

Reserved-Gate Picketing — The NLRB also has held that the boycott ban is violated where a union pickets a gate at an industrial plant that has been set aside for the exclusive use of neutral contractors and their employees. When the Supreme Court reviewed the decision, however, it added a qualification. It said that picketing of a reserved gate would not be unlawful if the work being done by the outside contractors using the gate was of a type previously done by the plant's own employees and was not *de minimis* in amount. (48 LRRM 2210, 51 LRRM 1028) The Board ruled, however, that this "normal-operations" test did not apply to picketing of a reserved gate at a construction project. Such picketing must meet the four tests for common-situs picketing (60 LRRM 1296). The Board's position has been upheld in the courts (66 LRRM 2294).

The Supreme Court held that a union did not violate the secondary boycott ban by picketing a gate to a railroad spur track owned by the railroad and adjacent to a struck plant. The gate was used exclusively by employees of the railroad. The picketing was protected primary activity, since it occurred at a situs proximate to and related to the day-to-day operations of the struck plant. (55 LRRM 2968)

In all of these boycotts cases, the Board will *not* consider the picketing a violation if the struck company and the picketed company have common ownership and control so that they are regarded as one "employer" under the law or if there is an ally relationship between the two. An ally relationship was found to exist in one case, for example, where the picketed companies "knowingly" were doing struck work and were being paid for doing it directly or indirectly by the struck company. (37 LRRM 2219)

HOT-CARGO CONTRACTS

As used by labor unions, the term "hot cargo" refers to goods produced or shipped by an "unfair" employer. In such a context, the term "unfair" may refer to a struck employer, to an employer whose goods bear no union label, or to an employer whose wages or other working conditions are deemed substandard by the union.

As a measure of self-protection, some unions have negotiated contracts giving their members the right to refuse to handle or process hot cargo. Prior to the 1959 amendments to the Act, hot-cargo agreements were not of themselves unlawful. But neither were they a defense to conduct otherwise within the reach of the secondary-boycott ban.

The 1959 amendments make it an unfair labor practice for an employer and a union to enter into any agreement under which the employer is to stop handling, selling, transporting, or using the products of any other person or to stop doing business with any other person. Agreements of this type previously entered into are made unenforceable and void.

The broad language used in the ban might encompass not only hot-cargo contracts but also various types of restrictions on subcontracting of work. There are specific exceptions for contracts dealing with jobbing and subcontracting in the clothing industry and job-site subcontracting in the construction industry, however. Moreover, the Supreme Court has held that the section does not outlaw contracts under which union members will not install prefabricated materials on construction jobs. (64 LRRM 2801, 64 LRRM 2821)

The theory of the Court in these cases involving installation of prefabricated materials was that the unions were enforcing work-preservation clauses designed to protect work that unit employees regularly and traditionally had performed. But the Board refused to apply the doctrine in a case in which it found the unit employees never had done the work involved, and there was no contract provision reserving such work for them. (69 LRRM 1344)

RIGHT-TO-CONTROL TEST

After the Supreme Court's decision on refusals to install prefabricated work on construction projects, there remained the issue as to whether the holding applied where the boycotted employer did not have the right to control the use of the prefabricated products on the construction. An example of such noncontrol would be where the specification to use the prefabricated material was made by others, such as the product owner or the general contractor. In cases involving the Plumbers and Carpenters Unions, the NLRB held that the work-preservation concept did not apply where the boycotted employer had no right to control the use of the prefabricated materials. (82 LRRM 1113, 82 LRRM 1119)

But three federal courts of appeals have disagreed with the NLRB's approach to the cases and the right-to-control exception. (67 LRRM 2532, 74 LRRM 2851, 69 LRRM 2858)

In late 1973, however, the Fourth Circuit adopted the NLRB's right-to-control test. It upheld a Board decision that two plumbers locals violated the Act by refusing to install prefabricated pipe because of a work-preservation clause in their contracts with a subcontractor. The court agreed with the Board that the primary employer did not have the legal "right to control" the disputed work.

RIGHTS OF STRIKERS

The Taft-Hartley Act's impact on strikes and picketing is two-sided. It makes certain types of strikes and picketing unlawful. But it also extends protection to employees to engage in certain strikes, picketing, and other concerted activities. The degree of protection, if any, depends on what type of strike is involved — economic, unfair-labor-practice, protected, unprotected, or illegal.

Unfair-Labor-Practice Strikes — The greatest degree of protection is extended to unfair-labor-practice strikes. An unfair-labor-practice strike is one caused or prolonged, in whole or in part, by unfair labor practices of the employer. Participants in such strikes are entitled to reinstatement in their jobs upon unconditional application, even though it may be necessary to discharge replacements to make room for them. Back pay also is customarily awarded from the time of an unconditional request for reinstatement. (1 LRRM 703)

Economic Strikes — The term "economic strike" has been used by the NLRB as a designation for any strike not caused or prolonged by unfair labor practices of the employer. The implication is that it is a strike to enforce economic demands. But the term also embraces a strike for recognition or organization. Economic strikers have only limited reinstatement rights. They may claim their former jobs if permanent replacements have not been hired. But prior to the strikers' application for reinstatement, the employer may protect his business by hiring replacements or by discontinuing jobs for business reasons. If permanent replacements are hired before the strikers apply for reinstatement, the employer may reject the strikers' applications without violating the law. (2 LRRM 610)

If an economic striker applies for a job as a new employee after the strike is over, the employer may not discriminate against him because of his participation in the strike. This would be an unfair labor practice. Moreover, the Supreme Court has held that an employer may not assure strike replacements some form of job tenure by granting them superseniority at the expense of the strikers. Such action is so inherently discriminatory and destructive of union activity, the Court said, as to violate the Act without regard to the employer's motivation. (53 LRRM 2121)

Economic strikers remain employees under the Act even after they have been replaced. So they are entitled to reinstatement as vacancies occur in their former jobs unless (1) they have obtained regular and substantially equivalent employment elsewhere in the meantime, or (2) the employer is able to establish legitimate and substantial business reasons to justify his failure to offer reinstatement. (66 LRRM 3727, 71 LRRM 3054)

Unprotected Strikes — Participants in unprotected strikes are not protected against discharge by their employer. Included in such strikes are not only those that are unlawful but also some not specifically forbidden by law. The penalty for an unprotected strike falls directly on the strikers, since they lose their reinstatement rights.

Unprotected strikes under the rulings of the courts and the Board include the following:

▶ Strikes that violate federal laws other than the Taft-Hartley Act, such as the laws against mutiny. (10 LRRM 544)

▶ Sit-down strikes. (4 LRRM 515)

▶ Strikes in violation of collective bargaining contracts. (4 LRRM 530)

▶ Slowdowns and partial strikes, such as a refusal to work overtime. (26 LRRM 1493, 19 LRRM 2008)

▶ Wildcat strikes in derogation of the bargaining agent's authority, as when a minority group of employees strikes to affect the course of negotiations without the union's authorization. (15 LRRM 580)

▶ A strike by a group of white employees to force their employer to fire all black employees. (27 LRRM 1442)

▶ A walkout during working hours for the purpose of attending a union meeting. (32 LRRM 1631)

▶ A strike for political reasons, such as a strike to put pressure on a state legislature to pass a bill supported by the union. (33 LRRM 2630)

▶ A strike to protest a foreman's demotion. The walkout was said to be in the interest of the foreman, rather than the employees. (20 LRRM 2321)

▶ "Hit-and-run" or intermittent strikes. (33 LRRM 1433)

▶ A strike in which a picket called customers crossing the picket line obscene names. The offending picket lost his protection under the Act. (64 LRRM 2385)

▶ A strike in which strikers engaged in violence against non-strikers. The loss of protection applied to the strikers who engaged in the violence. (64 LRRM 2724)

During the period of World War II wage and price controls, the NLRB held that employees who struck to compel their employer to give them a wage increase in excess of that allowed under the stabilization program lost their protection under the Act. So the employer was held not to have committed an unfair labor practice under the Act by discharging the strikers. (14 LRRM 64)

A similar case involving the Herman-dez Construction Company arose during the 1971-1973 controls. But the case was settled without litigation.

Under the wage-price controls of 1971-1973, a federal district court held that a company and a union both had violated the Economic Stabilization Act by putting into effect a wage increase in excess of the Pay Board's standards. The company had agreed to the increase under the pressure of a strike by the union, but it rolled back the increase during the hearing on the case. (20 WH Cases 939)

Strike During Cooling-Off Period — In an effort to encourage the resolution of contract disputes through bargaining, the Taft-Hartley Act lays down some strict procedures that must be followed before a party to a contract may engage in a strike or lockout over an attempt to modify or terminate a contract.

Before modifying or terminating a contract, a party must take these steps:

▶ A written notice must be served on the other party 60 days prior to the contract's expiration date or, if there is no expiration date, 60 days prior to the date on which it is proposed to modify or terminate the contract.

▶ An offer must be made to confer with the other party to negotiate the desired changes.

▶ The party must notify the Federal Mediation and Conciliation Service and any mediation agency within the state if the dispute still exists 30 days after the original notice was given to the other party.

▶ The moving party must permit the contract to continue in full force and effect, without resorting to strike or lockout, for 60 days after the original notice was given or until the expiration date of the contract, whichever occurs later.

Employees who strike during the 60-day cooling-off period forfeit their status as "employees" under the Act and are not protected against being discharged or otherwise disciplined by the employer for participating in the strike. This loss of protection, however, does not apply to a strike not involving "contract termination or modification." It has been held, for example, that the 60-day notice and cooling-off period does not apply to a strike caused by serious unfair labor practices of the employer not involving contract issues. (37 LRRM 2587)

STRIKES IN VIOLATION OF NO-STRIKE CLAUSES

The Norris-LaGuardia Act does not bar injunctive relief against a strike called by a union in violation of a no-strike clause in a collective bargaining contract where (1) the grievance leading to the strike was subject to arbitration under the contract; (2) the employer was ready to proceed with arbitration; and (3) the employer suffered irreparable injury from the breach of its no-strike obligation. (74 LRRM 2257) This 1970 Boys Markets holding overturned that of the Court in the 1962 Sinclair Refining case, in which the Court held that a no-strike clause could not be enforced in a suit brought under Section 301 of the Taft-Hartley Act. (50 LRRM 2420)

In a 1974 case, the Supreme Court upheld the jurisdiction of a state court to enjoin a work stoppage called in violation of a no-strike clause in a contract providing a binding settlement procedure, even though the strike arguably was an unfair labor practice under the Act's forced-work-assignment procedures. (86 LRRM 2212)

Federal Preemption — The basic principle involving federal preemption of state jurisdiction in picketing cases was enunciated in the 1959 Garmon case. The Supreme Court held that state jurisdiction must yield when conduct is "arguably" or "potentially" subject to the Taft-Hartley Act either as protected activity under Section 7 or as an unfair labor practice under Section 8. (49 LRRM 2838) The 1974 decision, however, limits the general principle where there is a no-strike clause and a dispute-settlement procedure in the contract.

A Teamsters Union local properly was enjoined from honoring a sister labor organization's picket line at another company under the Boys Markets principle, even though the union contended that its action was a sympathy strike. (87 LRRM 2044)

NATIONAL EMERGENCY STRIKES

There is another class of strikes that, although not unlawful in themselves, may be delayed or postponed under the Act. These are the so-called national-emergency strikes — those that affect an entire or substantial part of an industry and that, if permitted to occur, would in the opinion of the President imperil the national health or safety.

Such strikes may be postponed up to 80 days under a procedure entailing these steps: (1) appointment of a board of inquiry to report to the President the facts of the dispute, but without recommendations; (2) petition to a federal court for an injunction restraining the strike; (3) resumption of bargaining by the parties; (4) reconvening of the board of inquiry to report, 60 days after the issuance of an injunction, on the state of the negotiations and the employer's last offer; (5) publication of the report; (6) polling of the employees by the NLRB within the next 15 days as to acceptance of the employer's last offer; (7) petition for dissolution of the injunction at the close of 80 days; and (8) a report by the President to Congress, with recommendations.

A challenge to the constitutionality of these provisions and to an injunction issued under them in the 1959 basic steel strike was rejected by the Supreme Court. (45 LRRM 2066)

The Railway Labor Act also contains procedures for dealing with national emergency strikes, but it has been necessary for Congress to adopt *ad hoc* legislation requiring compulsory arbitration of disputes in the railroad industry. There have been many proposals in Congress to revise completely the rules dealing with national-emergency strikes.

THE RULES GOVERNING LOCKOUTS

A lockout is the term applied to an employer's action in temporarily closing his plant and laying off the workers during a labor dispute. It is often looked upon as the employer's counterpart of the union's strike weapon. And, like the strike, it is subject to some restrictions under the Taft-Hartley Act.

Under Section 7 of the Act, employees are guaranteed the right to engage in "concerted activities" for their mutual aid or protection. So an employer violates the Act when he locks out his employees for the purpose of defeating their organizational efforts or of impeding or discouraging other protected concerted activities. (30 LRRM 2529, 29 LRRM 2331)

Since a strike is among the "concerted activities" protected under the law, an employer who locks out his employees in anticipation of a strike commits an unfair labor practice unless unusual circumstances justify the action. Unusual circumstances that have been held to justify a lockout in anticipation of a strike include:

▶ A threatened strike at a bottling company would have resulted in a costly spoilage of syrup. (12 LRRM 151)

▶ A union refused to tell members of an auto dealers association when a threatened strike would occur, and the dealers needed advance notice to allow repair work in progress to be finished and returned to customers. (28 LRRM 1509)

▶ A lockout was necessary to avoid disruption of a department integrated with two others previously struck by the union and threatened with a new strike. (27 LRRM 1504)

▶ General contractors locked out their building trades employees after determining they couldn't continue operations without the striking members of the plumbing union. (32 LRRM 1374)

Bargaining Lockouts — The Supreme Court, moreover, has recognized the right of an employer to use a temporary lockout in support of legitimate bargaining objectives during contract negotiations.

The Court ruled that an employer does not violate the Act when, after an impasse has been reached in contract negotiations, he temporarily shuts down his plant and lays off his employees for the sole purpose of bringing economic pressure to bear in support of his legitimate bargaining position. (58 LRRM 2672)

The NLRB later ruled that a lockout invoked by a newspaper was lawful where (1) it was called under an agreement with another newspaper, (2) the two newspapers were engaged in simultaneous negotiations with the same union, and (3) an impasse was reached in negotiations at the second newspaper. (65 LRRM 1425)

In a later decision, the U.S. Court of Appeals for the District of Columbia upheld an NLRB decision that an employer did not violate the Act by locking out his employees *before* an impasse had been reached in negotiations in view of the following: (1) The lockout was not inherently destructive of employees' rights, and the employer had a legitimate and substantial business reason for the lockout. (2) The employer was not alleged to have any anti-union motive. (3) The employer engaged in 10 negotiating sessions before the lockout. (4) The union was strong, and the company had been organized for several years. (5) The employer had made numerous concessions during negotiations, and disagreement had been narrowed to a few items. (6) The major disagreement involved a work-assignment issue over which the employer had suffered a long strike earlier, and the union stated it was ready to strike over the issue "at a time of its choosing." And (7) the employer was engaged in a highly seasonal business, and had fear of "unusual harm" from a strike during the busy season. (68 LRRM 1133, 72 LRRM 2439)

A decision by the Seventh Circuit held that an employer association did not violate the Act's collective bargaining provisions when it locked out its members' employees more than 60 days after receiving a union's notification of an intention to modify the contract, but less than 30 days after the union's untimely notification to the federal and state mediation services. Reversing the NLRB's decision, the court said that by unlawfully prolonging its obligation to notify the mediation services and then subsequently notifying them at a propitious moment when the association had called for a lockout, the union, as the initiating party, skillfully could "manage to inflict liability for back-pay awards" on the employer. (86 LRRM 2914)

Multi-Employer Lockouts — Suppose a union, employing whipsawing tactics, strikes one member of a multi-employer bargaining group. May other members of the group counter the union's divide-and-conquer strategy by locking out their nonstriking employees?

In the leading case on this issue, the Supreme Court upheld such a defensive lockout by members of a multi-employer group. It considered the lockout as a justifiable measure to preserve the integrity of the bargaining unit in the face of the union's divide-and-conquer strategy. (39 LRRM 2603)

The Court also held in a subsequent case that members of a multi-employer bargaining group did not violate the Act by locking out their regular employees and using temporary replacements to continue operations in response to a whipsawing strike called by a union against one member of the group, who also continued operations with temporary replacements. (58 LRRM 2663)

CROSSING PICKET LINE

An employee has a right to honor a lawful picket line set up by his own union at his own plant, although if the strike is for economic reasons he may be permanently replaced, as discussed above. If the picket line is set up by another union representing other employees at the plant, however, the employee would not be protected by the Act against discipline or discharge if he refused, as a matter of principle, to cross the picket line. (28 LRRM 2079)

Where there is a lawful, authorized picket line at the plant of another employer, a proviso to the Act protects an employee against reprisal or discharge for refusing to cross the picket line, and the proviso has been held to validate contracts expressly permitting employees to decline to cross such picket lines in the course of their duties. But an employee loses that protection if there is a no-strike clause in the contract. Moreover, even without a no-strike clause, an employer is not barred from discharging the employees and replacing them with others willing to do the work in order to preserve the efficient operation of his business. (31 LRRM 2432, 54 LRRM 2707)

The Supreme Court held that a union did not violate the Act by imposing fines on members who crossed a lawful picket line set up by the union, demanding payment of the fines, and instituting court proceedings to collect them. The Court ruled that the union's action was not unlawful restraint or coercion of employees in the exercise of their right *not* to engage in concerted activities. (65 LRRM 2449)

Some of the questions left open by this decision were answered by the Supreme Court in two later decisions. The Court made these rulings:

▶ The NLRB does not have the authority to determine whether a fine lawfully imposed on a member for crossing a picket line is reasonable in amount. Such issues, the Court said, should be decided on the basis of the law of contracts, voluntary associations, or such other principles of law as may be applied in a forum competent to adjudicate the issue. State courts will be wholly free, under the Supreme Court's holding, to apply state law to such issues at the suit of either of the parties. (83 LRRM 2183) Thus the Wisconsin Supreme Court upheld a judgment in favor of a union involving a fine imposed on one of its members who crossed a picket line. (66 LRRM 2439)

▶ A union may not fine an employee who resigns from the union before crossing the union's picket line. But it may fine a member who does not resign from the union until after he crosses the picket line. (83 LRRM 2189, 2262)

See below under "Regulation of Unions" for a further discussion of this issue.

RACIAL-DISCRIMINATION PICKETING

An employer violated the Act by discharging two black employees who, independent of the union representing them, engaged in the concerted activity of picketing and distributing handbills to protest the employer's allegedly racially discriminatory employment practices, even though the union was trying to resolve the matter through the contractual grievance procedure. This did not deprive the conduct of the employees of its protected status under Section 7 of the Act. (83 LRRM 2738) This decision by the District of Columbia Circuit reversed a holding by the NLRB that the picketing lost its protected status when the employees failed to act through their collective bargaining representative. (77 LRRM 1669)

In an earlier decision, the Ninth Circuit applied the theory of the NLRB in the later case and held that picketing by employees to protest their employer's alleged racially discriminatory hiring practices lost its protected status under the Taft-Hartley Act when the employees failed to seek or obtain the sanction of their union. (72 LRRM 2866)

PICKETING AS FREE SPEECH

Peaceful picketing at a location generally open to the public is protected free speech under the First Amendment to the U.S. Constitution in the absence of other factors relating to the purpose or manner of the picketing. Applying this principle, the Supreme Court held that a state court violated the Constitution by enjoining a union's picketing in a parcel pick-up zone and parking lot in a shopping center. The Court said that the shopping center was the functional equivalent of the business district of a normal town and was open to the public to the same extent. (68 LRRM 2209)

The limitations of this doctrine were illustrated by the Supreme Court in a case involving an unfair-labor-practice charge filed by a union against a hardware company that owned and operated two retail stores located in large buildings surrounded on three sides by parking lots. The company had a no-solicitation rule applicable to the parking lots, and the union filed the charge when the company had a nonemployee organizer arrested for violating the no-solicitation rule. The Court ruled that the case was not governed by the free-speech doctrine enunciated in the prior case, but was governed by rules laid down under Section 7 of the Taft-Hartley Act. So the Supreme Court remanded the case to the court of appeals for reconsideration in the light of the principles laid down in the Babcock & Wilcox case (38 LRRM 2001) to the effect that an employer may bar nonemployee solicitation on its property where (1) the union may reach the employees through reasonable efforts through other available channels, and (2) the no-solicitation order does not discriminate against the union by allowing other solicitation or distribution. (80 LRRM 2769)

EXTORTIONATE PICKETING

A provision included in the 1959 Landrum-Griffin or Labor Reform Act that was not made a part of the Taft-Hartley Act makes it a federal crime for a union or individual to engage in "extortionate" picketing. This is defined as picketing for the personal profit or enrichment of any individual, except through a bona fide increase in wages or other employee benefits, by taking or obtaining any money or other thing of value from the employer against his will or without his consent.

SETTLEMENT OF DISPUTES

A measure of the successful conduct of labor relations is the degree in which disputes between management and employees are promptly and satisfactorily settled. Basically, there are two types of disputes. First, there are those involving conflicting management and union interests—those that are settled by the execution of a collective bargaining agreement. Second, there are disputes relating to rights under the contract. These usually are settled under the grievance procedure and, if that fails, by arbitration.

There are other types of disputes that affect labor relations. There are, for example, disputes between labor unions. These may be settled in a number of ways—by an impartial umpire or a joint board set up by the unions themselves, by the NLRB, or by the courts.

ROLE OF THE MEDIATION SERVICE

To provide assistance to management and labor in settling contract disputes, the Taft-Hartley Act set up a Federal Mediation and Conciliation Service. The duties of the Service in seeking to settle a dispute are outlined in the law as first conciliation, then mediation, and finally an effort to obtain consent for a vote by the employees on the employer's last offer. Conciliation is distinguished from mediation in that conciliation is the effort to get parties to agree to offers freely made by either side, while mediation entails suggestions by the third party of bases for settlement that had not been put forward by either side.

In addition to giving the FMCS these functions, the law requires that the Service be notified of all disputes over renewal or modification of contracts if no settlement has been reached 30 days after a desire for a change has been indicated. State mediation agencies must be notified at the same time. The Federal Service screens out cases that do not affect interstate commerce and those that affect it to a minor degree, leaving these to the state agencies to handle.

The FMCS also maintains a roster of arbitrators for referral to unions and employers. This will be discussed in more detail later.

Hospital Disputes — In 1974, Congress passed a law extending the coverage of the Taft-Hartley Act to private nonprofit hospitals and nursing homes. The NLRB previously had asserted jurisdiction over proprietary hospitals and nursing homes. (66 LRRM 1299, 66 LRRM 1264)

The new law establishes procedures that impose a heavy burden on the FMCS. It is estimated that the law brings 7,000 nonprofit hospitals and other health care institutions employing about 1.4 million employees under the Taft-Hartley Act.

The provisions of the Act and the new procedures apply equally to all proprietary and private nonprofit hospitals, convalescent hospitals, health maintenance organizations, health or medical clinics, nursing homes, extended care facilities, and other institutions devoted to the care of sick, infirm, or aged persons.

The dispute-settlement procedures under the law are as follows:

▶ Ninety days before contract termination, the union must notify the employer in writing.

▶ Sixty days before termination, the union must notify the FMCS that the existing contract will expire.

▶ Thirty days before termination, the Director of the FMCS may appoint a board of inquiry if he believes the negotiations are not moving well and an impasse could develop jeopardizing delivery of health-care services.

▶ Fifteen days before termination, the board makes its findings of fact and recommendations for settlement.

▶ Ten days before termination, the union must give notice to the employer that a strike seems imminent and that picketing may be expected.

In what amounts to a requirement of compulsory conciliation and mediation, the FMCS is mandated by the law, upon receiving the 60-day notice, to contact the parties in an effort to achieve a settlement. The parties are required to participate in meetings called by the FMCS. Within 30 days after receiving the 60-day notice, the FMCS may opt to invoke a 30-day "cooling-off" period if it determines that there is the likelihood of a strike or lockout that would "substantially interrupt the delivery of health care in the community."

This cooling-off procedure would involve the appointment of a board of inquiry to look into the facts of the dispute and report its findings and settlement recommendations to the parties. It would do so within 15 days of being created, with the parties having another 15 days to settle on the basis of the report.

Initial Bargaining — There is a different time schedule where the parties are bargaining for their first contract. The FMCS would receive only a 30-day notice of an existing dispute and its potential threat to health care delivery. The Service then would have only 10 days to opt to invoke the board-of-inquiry procedure. Again, if a board were appointed, it would have 15 days in which to compile the facts and issue recommendations for settlement, which would be made public.

Failure of the FMCS to settle a dispute relating to either an initial or a renewal contract within the required notice periods would not necessarily leave the union free to resort to self-help at once. Under a new Section 8 (g), a union must give the employer a 10-day notice of its intent to strike or picket — unless "flagrant" or "severe" unfair labor practices on the employer's part are involved. The delay is to enable the employer to make plans for the continuity of patient care.

In the case of disputes relating to an initial contract, the 10-day notice may not be served until the 30-day notice period has elapsed. So a union seeking an initial contract may not engage in strikes or picketing until 40 days following its notice to the FMCS that a dispute exists.

In disputes involving renegotiation of existing contracts, the parties have 15 days to settle on the basis of the report of the board of inquiry.

Preventive Mediation — The FMCS has increased its efforts in the area of preventive mediation — an effort at the parties' invitation to head off disputes before they occur. For this purpose, FMCS has created an Office of Technical Services to handle the preventive mediation function.

ARBITRATION OF DISPUTES

Just as commercial arbitration arose as a less expensive alternative to litigation, so labor arbitration has served as a less expensive alternative to a strike. It also may be resorted to as an alternative to a suit for breach of a collective bargaining contract.

When an employer and a union agree to arbitrate a dispute, each is giving up a right otherwise enjoyed. For example:

▶ *For the employer,* it means that he is giving up his right to take unilateral action on the matter under dispute.

▶ *For the union,* it means that it is giving up the right to strike over the issue submitted.

► *And for both,* it means that failure to abide by the decision of the neutral party empowered to decide the dispute could lead to a suit for enforcement of the award.

Arbitration proceedings usually begin with a submission agreement and the selection of an arbitrator. The submission agreement confers authority upon the arbitrator and defines the extent of that authority. If carefully drawn, the submission will state (1) the nature of the grievance, (2) the claim of the aggrieved party, (3) reference to the specific contract clause relied upon, (4) the relief sought, and (5) the retroactive or effective date of application of any award.

In some cases, the selection of an arbitrator is no problem. The contract between the employer and the union will designate a permanent umpire or arbitrator to handle all disputes arising under the contract. But under the majority of contracts, a temporary or *ad hoc* arbitrator must be selected for each dispute referred to arbitration.

Where a temporary arbitrator is to be used, the contracts usually specify alternative methods of selection. If the parties are unable to agree on an arbitrator within a specified period of time, the contract provides for designation of an arbitrator by an impartial agency. Most contracts designate either the Federal Mediation and Conciliation Service or the American Arbitration Association as the selecting agency.

Under the rules of the American Arbitration Association, the parties may make their own selection from lists provided by the Association. The parties may cross off names they object to, and the Association will choose from those remaining in order of preference. If no agreement can be reached on names on the lists, the Association will appoint an arbitrator not on the lists. (30 LA 1086)

The Federal Mediation and Conciliation Service also maintains a roster of experienced and qualified arbitrators from which the parties to a labor agreement may make their selection. Here again, the parties may select an arbitrator by striking those to whom they object from the list or by advising the FMCS of the order of preference among those on the panel. Beginning in late 1971, the FMCS began using a computer in the selection of panels.

ARBITRATION PROCEDURE

In a typical arbitration proceeding, the arbitrator communicates with the parties to arrange a hearing date. The parties may stipulate use of a specific hearing procedure, such as that suggested by the American Arbitration Association. Usually, however, the hearing procedure is determined by the arbitrator.

The formality of the hearing before the arbitrator will depend, in part, on the nature of the issues, the character of the parties, and the circumstances of the dispute. Formal hearings resembling legal trials sometimes are used, but most hearings are as informal as the orderly presentation of the evidence will allow.

In any case, all parties must be given an opportunity to be heard, which implies the right to receive notice of the hearing. If rights of a third party are involved, he should be given notice and opportunity to attend the hearing. The arbitrator has the responsibility of giving notice. The parties must be allowed to present evidence without unreasonable restriction and must be allowed to cross-examine adverse witnesses.

In a 1969 case, the U.S. Court of Appeals for the Second Circuit ruled that a federal district court had jurisdiction to order the consolidation of two arbitration cases involving the competing work claims of two unions. A key element in the holding was the presence in both union contracts of broad arbitration clauses permitting the employer to submit a grievance to arbitration. (72 LRRM 2140)

But the Fifth Circuit reversed a lower court decision enforcing an award issued by the union-appointed arbitrator acting alone. The contract permitted the arbitrator appointed by one party to arbitrate a grievance under certain conditions if the other party failed to appoint its representative. But the employer contended that he would not arbitrate the dispute until a court had determined the arbitratility of the dispute as a final matter. If there was arbitration, the employer added, his attorney would represent him. The court said it had a distaste for default arbitration, and so it construed the contract strictly to deny enforcement of the award issued by the union-appointed arbitrator. (83 LRRM 2298)

Arbitrators generally have wide discretion as to the observance of the rules of evidence. Neither the arbitrator nor the witnesses need be sworn unless required by a statute in the state. A majority of the states have some type of provision for the swearing of witnesses but not all make it compulsory upon the parties. The parties may make oral argument at the conclusion of the evidence, but they may waive the right. If the parties desire to file written briefs or if the arbitrator feels that it is desirable, briefs will be filed. The parties decide whether to have a written record of the hearing.

At the conclusion of the proceeding, the arbitrator renders an award that, by prior agreement of the parties, is final and binding.

NLRB'S DEFERRAL TO ARBITRATION

In the 1955 Spielberg case, the NLRB decided it would honor an arbitration award involving the same issue raised in a charge filed with the Board where (1) the arbitration proceedings appeared to have been "fair and regular," (2) all parties had agreed to be bound by the award, and (3) the arbitration decision was not clearly repugnant to the purposes and policies of the Act. The Board later added that the arbitrator must have considered the issue in the charge filed with the Board. (36 LRRM 1152)

But in 1974, the Board expanded the doctrine by holding that it will honor an arbitration award in a discharge or discipline case, even though the award gives no indication that the unfair labor practice issue before the Board was presented to the arbitrator or considered by him. In such situations, the Board said, it is sufficient that the issue could have been introduced before the arbitrator, but the party charging unlawful discrimination before the Board elected not to do so. (87 LRRM 1211)

The principle of honoring arbitration awards that meet the specified standards was extended to representation cases in the 1963 Raley's, Inc. decision. (53 LRRM 1347)

Collyer Doctrine — If a collective bargaining contract contains a grievance-arbitration procedure for resolving disputes under the contract, the NLRB will defer to the contractual procedure where an unfair-labor-practice charge also involving a contractual issue has been filed with the Board prior to arbitration. But the Board will retain jurisdiction over the dispute for the purpose of entertaining an appropriate and timely motion for further consideration upon a proper showing that either (a) the dispute has not been resolved either by amicable settlement in the grievance procedure with reasonable promptness after the Board's deferral decision or submitted promptly to arbitration or (b) the grievance or arbitration procedures have not been fair and regular or have reached a result that is repugnant to the Act. (77 LRRM 1931)

The Collyer case involved an alleged violation by the employer of his bargaining duty by taking unilateral action on a matter subject to bargaining. A similar holding was handed down in a 1972 case in which the employer unilaterally terminated a bonus. (81 LRRM 1402)

Another 1972 case involved both an alleged unlawful refusal to bargain and alleged unlawful discrimination. The Board deferred to arbitration under the collective bargaining contract on both issues. (80 LRRM 1718)

But the Board refused to defer to arbitration where the contract did not commit the employer and the union to binding third-party arbitration. (79 LRRM 1265) The decision was enforced by the Tenth Circuit. (84 LRRM 2300)

All of the Board's decisions in the deferral-to-arbitration cases have been by a margin of three-to-two where the full Board participated.

ARBITRATION AND CIVIL RIGHTS ACT

In a unanimous opinion, the Supreme Court held in 1974 that neither the doctrine of waiver nor the federal labor policy favoring arbitration bars a discharged employee whose claim of racial discrimination was rejected by an arbitrator from bringing an action on the same claim under Title VII of the Civil Rights Act of 1964. Moreover, the federal courts are not required to defer to the arbitrator's decision but, instead, should provide a trial *de novo* on the employee's claim. (7 FEP Cases 81)

The Court, however, pointed out that when an arbitration decision gives full consideration to Title VII rights, a court may give such a decision "great weight," particularly where the issue is solely one of fact and based on an adequate record.

ARBITRATION OF SAFETY DISPUTES

Under a collective bargaining contract containing an arbitration clause covering "any local trouble of any kind arising at the mine," the Supreme Court held, a dispute concerning the mine operator's continued employment of foremen who failed to carry out certain prescribed safety procedures was arbitrable. The presumption of arbitrability announced by the Supreme Court in the Steelworkers trilogy (46 LRRM 2416, 2414, 2423) applies to disputes over safety. (85 LRRM 2049)

In a case arising under the Fair Labor Standards Act, the Iowa Supreme Court held that employees engaged in interstate commerce are not required to use the grievance procedure, including arbitration, before suing for overtime pay under the Act. (10 WH Cases 488)

ARBITRATION OF NEW CONTRACTS

The arbitration of new-contract terms or "interest" arbitration has not been used to any extent in the private sector of the economy. But the Amalgamated Transit Union has engaged in such arbitration for 75 years, while the Printing Pressmen and Assistants' Union and the American Newspaper Publishers Association have a standard agreement for arbitration of new-contract disputes that cannot be settled by conciliation. Under the Experimental Negotiating Agreement between the Steelworkers and the basic steel companies, all issues not resolved by negotiations by a certain date are to be submitted to binding arbitration. In the 1974 negotiations, however, all issues were resolved by the parties. None were submitted to arbitration.

The public sector, in contrast, has used "interest" arbitration to a considerable extent. There also has been resort to fact-finding, with or without recommendations; final-offer arbitration, under which both parties submit final offers to a board of neutrals, which selects one as the final settlement; and "med-arb," under which the person selected by the parties tries first to resolve the dispute by mediation and then, if that fails, issues a binding arbitration award.

ENFORCEMENT OF ARBITRATION

At common law, an agreement to arbitrate, while not illegal, was revocable any time before rendition of the award and could not be specifically enforced in the courts. But this has been changed by Section 301 of the Taft-Hartley Act, which gives the federal district courts jurisdiction of suits for breaches of collective bargaining contracts.

In 1957, the U.S. Supreme Court ruled that this Section 301 gives the federal courts jurisdiction to order the performance of employer-union contracts to arbitrate disputes.

As a follow-up to this decision, the Supreme Court since has laid down some rules to guide the federal courts in enforcing both arbitration agreements and arbitration awards. In brief, the rules are as follows:

▶ Unless the contract specifies otherwise, an employee must attempt to use the grievance-arbitration procedure of the union contract in pressing a grievance before resorting to the courts. (58 LRRM 2193)

▶ The question of the arbitrability of a dispute is for the courts to decide, unless the parties clearly state to the contrary. (46 LRRM 2410)

▶ This, however, does not give the courts authority to decide questions of contract interpretation or application. The parties agreed to let arbitrators pass on the merits of a dispute because they believed arbitrators are better equipped to perform this task than are the courts; the parties' wishes should be respected. Moreover, questions of "procedural arbitrability," such as whether the grievance procedure has been complied with, are so intertwined with the merits that they also are for the arbitrator to decide. (46 LRRM 2410, 55 LRRM 2769)

▶ When a party seeks enforcement of an arbitration clause, the court's only job is to determine whether the contract contains a promise to arbitrate the dispute. A court may not refuse to order arbitration merely because it considers a grievance baseless. (46 LRRM 2414)

▶ A court may not modify or refuse to enforce an arbitration award merely because it disagrees with the arbitrator's interpretation of the contract. If the parties agree to make arbitration final and binding, the courts should not substitute their judgment for that of the arbitrator. (46 LRRM 2423)

▶ Although state courts have concurrent jurisdiction with the federal courts over actions brought under Section 301 of the Taft-Hartley Act to enforce collective bargaining contracts, the state courts must apply federal law wherever there is a conflict. (49 LRRM 2619, 49 LRRM 2717)

▶ If a union has agreed to submit a certain type of dispute to final and binding arbitration, it violates the contract if it strikes over such a dispute. It is not necessary that the contract contain an express no-strike pledge. (49 LRRM 2717)

▶ But a work stoppage in violation of a collective bargaining contract does not necessarily give the employer the right to refuse to arbitrate the grievance that caused the stoppage of work. The operation of the grievance-arbitration provisions of the contract is not dependent upon the union's observance of the no-strike clause. The employer may sue for damages in a federal district court. (55 LRRM 2580)

▶ Moreover, if a union strikes in violation of a no-strike clause in a collective bargaining contract, a federal district court has jurisdiction to issue an order enjoining the strike where (1) the grievance leading to the strike is subject to arbitration under the contract, (2) the employer is ready to proceed with arbitration, and (3) the employer suffered irreparable injury from the union's breach of its no-strike obligation. This decision in the 1970 Boys Markets case overturned the holding of the Supreme Court in the 1962 Sinclair Refining case. (74 LRRM 2257)

▶ A damage action brought by an employer for a union's alleged breach of a no-strike contract may not be dismissed or stayed pending arbitration where the contract limits arbitration to employee grievances. But such an action should be stayed pending arbitration where the arbitration clause in the contract is sufficiently broad to cover the claim. (50 LRRM 2433, 50 LRRM 2440)

▶ The courts may enforce arbitration in suits brought under Section 301 even though the conduct involved also may be an unfair labor practice within the NLRB's jurisdiction (55 LRRM 2042). Moreover, the NLRB will honor arbitration awards in both unfair-practice and representation cases, provided certain standards are met (36 LRRM 1152, 53 LRRM 1347).

If a collective bargaining contract contains a grievance-arbitration procedure for resolving disputes under the contract, the NLRB will defer to the contractual procedure where an unfair-labor-practice charge also involving a contractual issue has been filed with the Board prior to arbitration. After the award has been issued by the arbitrator, the Board will review it to determine whether it meets its standards for honoring awards. (77 LRRM 1931)

An arbitration award that a union's grievance relating to recall of strikers was not arbitrable could not be vacated by a court where there was no error either in the arbitrator's conclusions or in the procedure by which he reached those conclusions. The parties had agreed to submit the issue of arbitrability to the arbitrator. (62 LRRM 2011)

An arbitrator did not exceed his authority when he excluded polygraph (lie-detector) tests in determining whether an employer had proper cause for discharging two employees suspected of theft. Under the contract, the employer reserved the right to require lie-detector tests of any employee suspected of theft. But the court pointed out that the contract made no mention of the use of such tests in arbitration. Moreover, such tests may be useful in other ways, including preliminary investigation. The arbitrator has great flexibility on the admissibility of evidence, and the court should not review the legal adequacy of his evidentiary rulings, particularly on lie-detector tests — an issue even the courts have found debatable. (83 LRRM 2652)

An arbitrator exceeded his authority in deciding that an employer's past practice of granting employees paid voting time or one hour off on election day was continued during the current contract as an implied condition in view of the employer's failure to negotiate a contrary policy into the contract. (62 LRRM 2495)

State Arbitration Laws — Many of the states have arbitration statutes that set up guides for court review of arbitration awards. Under these laws, an award may be set aside by a court only if there is fraud, bias, misconduct by the arbitrator, or a decision that goes beyond the scope of the submission. Because of the broad latitude given arbitrators by the Supreme Court's decisions under Section 301 of the Taft-Hartley Act, however, it is likely that most future suits to compel arbitration or enforce arbitration awards will be filed in the federal courts.

REGULATION OF UNIONS

Until the adoption of the Landrum-Griffin Act in 1959, Congress had adhered to the view that the Federal Government should not interfere with the internal affairs or organization of labor unions. The courts, both state and federal, had demonstrated a similar aversion to direct intervention in intra-union affairs.

The 1959 Landrum-Griffin or Labor-Management Reporting and Disclosure Act changed all this. It put the Federal Government in the business of policing the internal affairs of labor organizations — local unions as well as national and international bodies. The regulation it provides for is minute in detail. There are detailed informational and financial reporting requirements. There is a bill of rights for union members. There are procedural requirements a union must satisfy before it may raise dues or fees. There is a guarantee of a union member's right to sue the union. There are standards for disciplinary proceedings within the union. There are restrictions on trusteeships. There are rules for the conduct of union elections. Obligations are placed upon union officers and employees, employers, and labor relations consultants. And the statutory requirements have been supplemented by decisions of the courts and regulations and interpretations of the Labor Department's Office of Labor-Management and Welfare-Pension Reports.

These rules are summarized and explained below.

REPORTING REQUIREMENTS

Labor organizations are required to file two types of reports under the Act. First, every union must adopt a constitution and bylaws and file a copy with the Secretary of Labor. In addition, the union must file a detailed statement of its provisions and procedures with regard to a number of other matters, provided they are not covered in the constitution and bylaws. These include:

▶ The initiation fee or fees required from a new or transferred member. In a case involving a local of the Plumbers Union, an appeals court upheld a lower court decision requiring the local to accept transfer of the membership of an employee to the local and awarding the aggrieved member damages for loss of wages, damage to his reputation, and humiliation and embarrassment. (84 LRRM 2266)

▶ Fees for work permits and the regular dues or fees required to remain a member.

▶ Qualifications for or restrictions on membership; participation in insurance or other benefit plans.

▶ Assessments.

▶ Authorization for disbursement of funds; financial audits.

▶ The calling of meetings.

▶ Method of selecting stewards, officers, and delegates, with specific information as to how each present officer got his job.

▶ Discipline or removal of officers for misconduct.

▶ Procedure and grounds for imposing fines, suspensions, or expulsions on members.

▶ Authorization for bargaining demands; ratification of contract terms.

▶ Strike authorizations.

▶ Issuance of work permits.

Besides filing all of this information with the Secretary of Labor, a union must make the information available to all of its members. Moreover, it must allow any member who has "just cause" to examine the union's books and records to verify the report.

Financial Reports—The second type of report a union must file under the law is a financial report. Such a report must be filed once a year within 90 days after the close of the union's fiscal year. The report must be signed by the union's president and treasurer and must give the following financial information in reasonable detail:

▶ Assets and liabilities at the beginning and the end of the year.

▶ All receipts and their sources.

▶ Salaries and all other payments to officers and to any employee who received more than $10,000 in total from the union and any of its affiliates.

▶ Complete information on any loans totaling more than $250 to any officer, employee, or member.

▶ Complete information on any direct or indirect loans to any business.

▶ Other disbursements and the reasons for them.

The Department of Labor has issued forms which the unions can use in filing both the information and the financial reports.

There are two financial report forms — a regular one and a short and simplified form for small unions. (See LRX 7105, 7125.)

The Secretary of Labor may bring civil actions to compel compliance with the reporting requirements. There are criminal penalties for willful violations. Supporting records must be kept available for inspection for five years.

UNION MEMBERS' BILL OF RIGHTS

In adopting the union members' bill of rights in the Landrum-Griffin Act, Congress attempted to legislate into the internal laws and procedures of unions the essential guarantees of the Bill of Rights of the Constitution of the United States.

In brief, here is what the provisions seek to guarantee:

Equal Rights—Subject to "reasonable rules and regulations," all union members have equal rights (1) to nominate candidates for union office; (2) to vote in elections or referenda; (3) to attend meetings; and (4) to discuss and vote on matters that come up in union meetings. A union member is defined as anyone who has fulfilled the requirements prescribed by the union for membership. (47 LRRM 2734)

Freedom of Speech and Assembly—This protects the right of members who are opposed to an incumbent administration in a union to meet and make plans to make their opposition effective. Here again, however, the right is subject to "reasonable rules" of the union. It has been held by federal courts of appeals that this section protects a member against discipline for expressing his opinion about the union's officers and policies, even if his statements are false. (52 LRRM 2908, 58 LRRM 2125, 59 LRRM 2821) In a case involving the Seafarers Union that went to the Supreme Court, the right of a member to reinstatement was upheld as furthering not only his right of free speech under the Act but also that of the union and other members. The member had been expelled for introducing a resolution containing derogatory remarks before the union membership. (83 LRRM 2177)

Dues, Initiation Fees, and Assessments—Before either a local or an international union may raise dues, fees, or assessments, certain procedural safeguards must be met. In a local, the increase must be approved by majority vote in either a special membership meeting or in a membership referendum. Both must be by secret ballot. National and international unions may increase dues, fees, and assessments by majority vote in a regular or special convention, by a secret-ballot referendum of the membership, or by majority executive board vote — to be effective until the next convention. In a case involving the Railway Clerks, whose constitution requires that a dues increase be approved by a two-thirds vote at the convention, an appeals court held the case should be sent back for trial on the basis of affidavits that the vote was taken first by a show of hands and then by a standing vote. No attempt was made in either instance to determine the exact division. (84 LRRM 3476)

Protection of the Right To Sue—Although a member still must utilize the union's internal procedures before taking a complaint to court, he need do so for only four months. But the exhaustion of the union's internal procedures was not required by an appeals court where it found that such action would have been futile since the union already had disciplined other members for the same action—crossing a picket line of another union. (84 LRRM 2791) The same section also declares a union member to be free "to petition any legislature or to communicate with any legislator."

Safeguards Against Improper Disciplinary Action—Except for failure to pay his dues, no union member may be subjected to discipline by fine, suspension, or expulsion unless he is (1) served with written, specific charges, (2) given a reasonable time to prepare his defense, and (3) afforded a full and fair hearing. There have been a number of court decisions dealing with what constitutes a "full and fair hearing" under the Act. In a case involving an independent union, a court set aside the suspension of the union president from membership and from office where the action was taken by the union's executive council, most of whose members were political opponents of the suspended president. (84 LRRM 2105) In another case, however, the expulsion of the president of a local for advocating disaffiliation from the international union and using union money for that purpose was upheld by a court. The court found that the charges against the local president were stated in detail and that he failed to attend the hearing, relying on free speech to justify his action. (84 LRRM 2569)

Union members may enforce these rights by civil suits in the federal courts. A union member also has a right to obtain a copy of a collective bargaining contract directly affecting his rights. The Secretary of Labor may enforce this right by a civil suit.

UNION ELECTIONS

National and international unions now are required to elect officers at least once every five years, either by secret ballot among the members or at a convention of delegates chosen by secret ballot. Local unions must elect officers at least once every three years by secret ballot. Officers of intermediate bodies, such as joint councils, must be elected at least once every four years by secret ballot or by delegates who, themselves, were elected by secret ballot.

The Landrum-Griffin Act also lays down some ground rules for the conduct of union elections. Here are some of them:

▶ A union must comply with any reasonable request by a candidate to distribute campaign literature to members by mail. It cannot discriminate among candidates as to the use of its membership lists for campaign purposes.

▶ A union may not use money from dues or assessments to promote the candidacy of any person running for office in a union. Moreover, no money of any employer is to be used for this purpose. But the union may use its money for notices and factual statements of issues not involving candidates and for other election expenses.

▶ Reasonable opportunity must be given for the nomination of candidates, and the union must provide adequate safeguards to assure a fair election, including the right of any candidate to have an observer at the polls and at the counting of ballots.

▶ Elections must be conducted in accordance with the union's constitution and bylaws, and ballots and election records must be preserved for a year.

▶ Every member of the union in good standing is entitled to vote and to support candidates of his choice without being subject to penalty, discipline, or reprisal of any kind by the union or any of its members. To be in good standing, a member must have fulfilled the membership requirements, must not have withdrawn voluntarily, and must not have been expelled or suspended in valid proceedings.

▶ Where officers are elected by delegates at a convention, the union's constitution and bylaws must be observed, and all convention records relating to the election, including credentials of delegates, must be preserved for a year.

Elections in two major unions, the Electrical Workers (IUE) and the United Mine Workers (Ind.), were set aside and different candidates declared elected by action of the Labor Department because of failure to abide by these ground rules.

ENFORCEMENT OF ELECTION RULES

Up to the point where an election is held, the provisions of state and local laws may be invoked to enforce any rights or remedies that may be available to a member under the union's constitution and bylaws. But once an election has been held, only a union member may initiate an attack on its validity. The Landrum-Griffin Act sets forth a procedure for challenging an election, including a challenge based on alleged infringement of the right to nominate candidates, and it specifies that the remedy thus provided shall be "exclusive." This is the procedure:

▶ The member first must proceed through the channels provided by the constitution and bylaws of the union and its parent body. But if the internal union procedures do not conform to the requirements of the Act, a court may order a new election. This was done in an election involving a Teamsters local where the union failed to mail a notice of the election to 58 percent of its membership, and only 23 percent of the membership voted. (85 LRRM 2594) In another case, involving the United Mine Workers, the court found that unfairness was built into the procedures established by the union's constitution. The incumbent officers were permitted to retain custody of and count the ballots. (83 LRRM 2352) In a case involving the Hotel, Motel & Club Employees, the Supreme Court held in 1966 that a bylaw limiting eligibility for major elective office to members who hold or have held elective office was not a "reasonable qualification." The rule disqualified 93 percent of the membership. (68 LRRM 2305)

▶ The union has three months to handle the complaint. If the union hasn't acted within that time or if it has acted and the member is not satisfied, he can complain to the Secretary of Labor. He must do so within a month.

▶ The Secretary then must investigate the member's charges. If he finds "probable cause" to believe that a violation of the law has occurred and it has affected the result of the election, the Secretary then brings suit against the union and asks the court to order a new election.

▶ If an election is directed by the court, it then is held under the supervision of the Secretary, who certifies to the court the persons elected. The court then enters a decree declaring them elected.

The Supreme Court held that a challenge to the union's rules on nomination of candidates was subject to this procedure; the member could not sue on his own. (57 LRRM 2561)

REMOVAL OF UNION OFFICERS

The Landrum-Griffin Act places initial reliance on the constitution and bylaws of the local union to provide procedures for the removal of union officers. But the law also instructs the Secretary of Labor to issue rules and regulations prescribing minimum standards and procedures for determining the adequacy of local union removal standards.

The policing of the adequacy of the removal procedures rests with the members of the union. But any member may invoke the aid of the Secretary of Labor in this respect.

The Secretary then is to provide a hearing on the matter. If he finds that the procedures are inadequate for the removal of an elected official guilty of serious misconduct, the official then becomes removable.

Actual removal of an officer has to be accomplished by an election conducted in accordance with the union's constitution and bylaws insofar as they are not inconsistent with the requirements of the Act. Before the election is held, cause must be shown for the officer's removal, and he must be given notice and hearing.

BAN ON FORMER CONVICTS, COMMUNISTS

The Landrum-Griffin Act also places some limitations on who may be a union officer or employee. Certain ex-convicts are barred from holding any office or job, other than strictly clerical or custodial, either with a union or an employer association. They also are barred from serving as a labor relations consultant. Here are the rules:

Ex-Convicts—Persons convicted of the following crimes are barred from holding union office for a five-year period: robbery, bribery, extortion, embezzlement, grand larceny, burglary, arson, violation of the narcotics laws, murder, rape, assault that inflicts grievous bodily injury, or violation of the law's reporting or trusteeship requirements. The five-year period runs from the end of the person's imprisonment or from the end of his parole following imprisonment.

The five-year ban for an ex-convict may be lifted, however, if either (1) his citizenship rights, revoked as a result of the conviction, are subsequently fully restored, or (2) the Justice Department's Board of Parole determines that it would not be contrary to the purposes of the law if the individual were permitted to hold office.

Communists—Under Section 504 of the Landrum-Griffin Act, it was made a crime for a person to hold union office during or for five years after termination of his membership in the Communist Party. This section of the Act was held unconstitutional by the Supreme Court in June 1965 in the Brown case. (59 LRRM 2353)

RULES ON UNION TRUSTEESHIPS

Most union constitutions contain procedures for placing local unions under a trusteeship supervised by the parent body. The Landrum-Griffin Act, however, placed some strict controls on such trusteeships.

In the first place, a parent organization that places a local or other subordinate body under trusteeship must file a report on the trusteeship with the Labor Department within 30 days. Thereafter, a report must be filed every six months while the trusteeship remains in effect. Among other things, these reports must give a detailed statement of the reasons for the trusteeship and a full and complete account of the trusteed organization's financial condition when the trusteeship was imposed.

There also are some limitations on the purposes for which a trusteeship may be established. The trusteeship may be imposed only in accordance with the parent organization's constitution and bylaws and only for these purposes:

▶ Correcting corruption or financial malpractice.

▶ Assuring the performance of collective bargaining agreements or other duties of a collective bargaining representative.

▶ Restoring democratic procedures.

▶ Otherwise carrying out the legitimate objectives of the local.

Unlawful Acts Under Trusteeship—There are certain actions that are forbidden while a subordinate labor organization is under trusteeship. It is unlawful, for example, to count the votes of delegates of a trusteed union in a convention of the parent body unless the delegates have been selected by secret ballot in an election in which all members in good standing of the trusteed union were eligible to vote.

It also is unlawful to transfer to the parent body any current receipts or other funds of the trusteed union, except the normal per capita tax and assessments normally payable.

Enforcement of Trusteeship Rules—The Act provides two methods of enforcing the trusteeship requirements.

▶ A complaint may be made to the Secretary of Labor who, if he finds probable cause to believe a violation has occurred and has not been remedied, may bring a civil suit in federal court for such relief as may be appropriate. In such cases, the identity of the complainant is not disclosed.

▶ A union member or subordinate body "affected by any violation" may bring a civil action for appropriate relief, including an injunction.

In these suits, one of the major considerations will be the length of time the trusteeship has been in effect. If it has been in existence for less than 18 months, it is presumed valid, and relief will be granted only upon "clear and convincing proof" that it was not established or maintained in good faith for a permissible purpose.

But if the trusteeship has been in effect for more than 18 months, the burden shifts and the trusteeship is presumed invalid. The court will decree termination of the trusteeship unless it is shown by "clear and convincing proof" that continuation is necessary for an allowable purpose.

In a case growing out of the 1972 presidential campaign, the AFL-CIO imposed a trusteeship on the Colorado Labor Council because it had endorsed Senator George McGovern, contrary to the AFL-CIO's policy of neutrality. In upholding the trusteeship, an appeals court ruled that the council was not a labor organization within the meaning of the Act and so the trusteeship provisions were not applicable. (83 LRRM 2361)

RESPONSIBILITIES OF UNION OFFICERS

The corrupt practices and wrongdoing of some union officials disclosed by the McClellan Committee hearings led Congress to include in the Landrum-Griffin Act provisions imposing a high standard of responsibility on union officials. The Act states that the "officers, agents, shop stewards, and other representatives" of a union occupy positions of trust in relation to the union and its members. The Act then specifies three areas in which union officers may be held accountable:

Union Funds—Union officers are required to hold, invest, and expend the union's money and property solely for the benefit of the union and its members. Embezzlement of union funds by either a union officer or a union employee is a federal crime punishable by fine, imprisonment, or both. (See below.)

Conflicts of Interest—Union officers are required to refrain from dealing with the union in an adverse capacity or on behalf of an adverse party in any matter connected with their duties as officers. There also is a breach of trust where a union officer has an investment or other financial or personal interest that conflicts with the interest of the union.

Exploiting the Office—A union officer is required to account to the union for any profits reaped while using his office, although not union funds, to his personal advantage. This type of exploitation is not made a breach of trust, since only an accounting is required. But if the accounting disclosed a conflict of interest, a breach of the fiduciary duty then would be found.

The enforcement of these provisions is left to the union members. As a first step, the member has to complain to the union about an officer's alleged breach of trust. If, after a reasonable time, the union doesn't do anything about the matter, the member may go into court—state or federal—and ask for leave to sue. If the member shows that he has complied with the law's requirements and shows good cause, he may sue the union officer.

If the officer is charged with having used his office for personal advantage, the member apparently is limited to requesting an accounting. But if the officer allegedly misappropriated union funds or became involved in a conflict-of-interest situation, the member may seek damages or other appropriate relief, including an injunction. (55 LRRM 2060)

BONDING, EMBEZZLEMENT, LOANS

In addition to imposing a fiduciary responsibility on union officers, the Landrum-Griffin Act also established new rules relating to bonding of union officers and employees, embezzlement of union funds, and loans to union officers. In brief, these are the rules:

▶ Bonding is required for every officer, agent, shop steward, employee, or other representative of a union who handles funds or other property. The bond may be the typical commercial honesty bond. Bonding also is required for officers or employees of employee-benefit funds in which the union "is interested."

▶ Embezzlement of union funds by a union officer is made a federal offense punishable by a fine of not more than $10,000 or imprisonment for not more than five years, or both. Embezzlement by union employees also is made a criminal offense, although the law does not cover the embezzlement of trust funds in which the union is interested. It also is made a federal offense to use force or threats of force against union members to interfere with the exercise of any of their rights under the Act.

▶ Loans by a union, directly or indirectly, to either officers or employees of the union are forbidden if they result in a total indebtedness of more than $2,000. Moreover, a union may not pay the fine of any officer or employee convicted of willfully violating the statute; nor may union funds be used to pay the legal fees of officers charged with misappropriating union funds, although the union would have the power to give financial support to an officer where a suit against him would have a direct and injurious effect upon the union itself. (47 LRRM 2040)

REPORTS BY UNION OFFICERS

The Landrum-Griffin Act also requires union officers and employees to file reports with the Labor Department on certain financial holdings and transactions. The reports must be filed annually within 90 days of the end of the fiscal year in which the transaction occurred. They must cover not only the official or employee, but also his wife and minor children, and they must describe:

▶ Any stock or other financial interest in any company represented or being organized by the union.

▶ Any payment or benefit from the company other than wages and benefits earned as a bona fide employee.

▶ Any transaction involving the stock or other financial interest in the company.

▶ Any stock or other financial interest in a company that does a substantial part of its business with an employer represented by or being organized by the union, and any income or other benefits received from such a company.

▶ Any stock or other financial interest in a company that deals in any way with the union.

▶ Any business transaction or arrangement with a company represented or being organized by the union, except pay for bona fide employment or purchases or sales in the normal course of business at regular prices.

▶ Payments or other benefits received from a labor relations consultant, other than specified permitted payments for legitimate purposes.

Exceptions—There are exceptions for bona fide investments in securities traded on a registered national exchange and in shares of registered investment companies and public utility holding companies. No report is required if the officer and his family had no dealings of the kind listed.

Enforcement—The Secretary of Labor is empowered to enforce these requirements by civil actions in the federal courts. There are criminal penalties for willful violations. Records supporting a report must be maintained available for inspection for five years.

RESTRICTIONS ON EMPLOYERS, CONSULTANTS

The same McClellan Committee hearings that uncovered corrupt practices on the part of some union officials also uncovered wrongdoing by some employers and so-called labor relations middlemen in their relations with unions and employees. In an effort to curb these practices, the Landrum-Griffin Act placed some new restrictions on the activities of employers and labor relations consultants.

The new restrictions on employers relate primarily to certain payments to employees and to union officers or agents. Some types of payments are made illegal, and employers also are required to file reports with the Secretary of Labor regarding certain payments and arrangements.

Unlawful Payments—Section 302 of the Taft-Hartley Act made it unlawful for an employer to make payments, with certain exceptions, to "any representative of any of his employees." It also was made unlawful for the representative to demand or accept such payments.

The Landrum-Griffin Act broadened these provisions considerably. The ban was expanded to include payments made by employer associations, labor relations consultants acting for an employer, and anyone else who acts in the employer's interest. It also was broadened to include loans or agreements to lend, as well as payments of money or any other thing of value.

Under the Taft-Hartley Act, only payments to a representative of the employer's employees were unlawful. Now the category of recipients has been expanded so that payments or loans are unlawful if they go to any of the following:

▶ Any representative of the employer's employees.

▶ Unions and union officers or employees where the union is seeking to represent the employer's employees or would admit them to membership.

▶ Any union officer or employee if the employer's intent is to influence him in respect to any of his actions or decisions as a union officer or employee.

▶ Individual employees or employee committees if (1) the payment is in excess of the employee's normal compensation and (2) it is for the purpose of causing the employee or employee committee, directly or indirectly, to influence other employees with respect to their organizing or bargaining rights.

Exempted Payments—There are a number of specific exemptions from this ban on employer payments or loans. They include: (1) compensation paid to a union officer or employee by reason of his services as an employee of the employer and payments to any employee whose duties include acting openly for the employer in labor relations or personnel matters; (2) payments to satisfy or settle a legal judgment, administrative agency order, or arbitration award; (3) the purchase of an article at the prevailing market price; (4) the deduction and payment over of union dues pursuant to a checkoff agreement; (5) payments into an employee-benefit trust fund that meets certain specifications; and (6) payments to a trust fund established for the purpose of pooled vacation, holiday, severance, or similar benefits or to defray the costs of apprenticeship or other training programs, provided certain conditions are met.

REPORTING REQUIREMENTS

Unlike unions, employers are not required by the Landrum-Griffin Act to file any regular reports with the Labor Department. They must file reports only if they make certain payments or enter into certain arrangements. The reports are due within 90 days after the end of the employer's fiscal year in which the payments or arrangements were made.

A report is required on any of the following kinds of transactions or arrangements:

▶ Payments or loans to any union or its representative, except those made by a bank, credit union, or other lending agency and those — such as normal wages — that are permitted by the unlawful payment provisions.

▶ Secret payments to certain employees to get them to persuade other employees on matters of organizing or bargaining.

▶ Expenditures intended to interfere with the right of employees to bargain freely.

▶ Expenditures for information on activities of employees or a union in connection with a labor dispute involving the employer, except for use in a proceeding before an arbitrator, administrative agency, or a court.

▶ Any arrangement with a labor consultant or other outsider where an object is to persuade employees with respect to organizing or collective bargaining.

▶ Any arrangement with a labor consultant or other outsider where an object is to get information on the activities of employees or a union in connection with a labor dispute involving the company, except for use in a proceeding before an arbitrator, administrative agency, or court.

▶ Any payment made pursuant to such arrangements with consultants or other outsiders.

Reports by Consultants—The reporting requirements with respect to the last three types of arrangements and payments listed above are two-edged. The consultant, as well as the employer, must file a report on the arrangement or payment. The consultant's report on an arrangement or agreement must be filed within 30 days after it is made. Reports on payments or disbursements under an arrangement must be filed annually.

The consultant, however, need not file reports for the following types of services: (1) giving of advice to an employer; (2) representing an employer before a court, administrative agency, or arbitration tribunal; and (3) negotiating bargaining agreements or grievances. Furthermore, attorneys need not report information lawfully communicated to them by clients in the course of a legitimate attorney-client relationship.

The Labor Department, however, has taken the position that where an attorney, or consultant, enters into any arrangement during a year to persuade employees with respect to organizing or collective bargaining, he must file a report on all income and expenditures during the year in connection with labor relations advice and services, not merely those related to the persuasion activities. This view has been upheld by a federal court of appeals. (60 LRRM 2264) The decision was denied review by the U.S. Supreme Court. (61 LRRM 2376)

Enforcement—The Secretary of Labor may bring a civil action in court whenever it appears that any employer or consultant has violated or is about to violate the reporting requirements. There are criminal penalties for willful violations. All of the reports required under the law — from unions, union officers, employers, and consultants — are available for inspection by interested persons at the Labor Department. Records supporting the reports must be kept available for inspection for five years.

ADMINISTRATION OF ACT

Shortly after the Act was adopted, a Bureau of Labor-Management Reports was established in the Labor Department to administer the law's provisions. In 1963, however, a new Office of Labor-Management and Welfare-Pension Reports was created, and this Office was given the responsibility for administering both the Labor-Management Reporting and Disclosure Act and the Welfare and Pension Plans Disclosure Act.

TAFT-HARTLEY ACT RESTRICTIONS

It is an unfair labor practice under the Taft-Hartley Act for a union to restrain or coerce employees in the exercise of their rights under the Act, including the right to refrain from union or concerted activities. In a series of decisions construing this prohibition, the Supreme Court and the NLRB have laid down the following rules:

▶ A union did not violate the Act by imposing fines on members who crossed a lawful picket line set up by the union and by instituting a legal proceeding to collect the fines. (65 LRRM 2449) (See "Strikes, Picketing, Boycotts, and Lockouts" for further rulings on this point.)

But a union did violate the Act by fining employees who had been members in good standing, but who resigned during a lawful strike called by the union and then crossed the picket line and returned to work, according to the Supreme Court ruling. (81 LRRM 2853) In a companion case, the Supreme Court also held that the NLRB does not have authority to determine whether a fine lawfully imposed upon a member is "reasonable" in amount. That is a matter for the state courts to determine. (81 LRRM 2183)

▶ A union did not violate the Act by fining members for drawing immediate piecework pay for work in excess of a production ceiling initiated by the union. (70 LRRM 3105)

▶ A union violated the Act by expelling a member for failure to exhaust the intra-union grievance procedure before filing an unfair-labor-practice charge against the union with the NLRB. (68 LRRM 2257)

▶ A union did not violate the Act by suspending from membership for five years a member who had filed a petition with the NLRB to decertify the union as bargaining representative. But a union did violate the Act when it fined, rather than suspended or expelled, a member who had filed a petition to decertify the union. (58 LRRM 1330, 64 LRRM 2495, 72 LRRM 1049)

HOW TO USE THE TAFT-HARTLEY ACT

How may employees, unions, or employers who believe their rights under the law have been violated obtain redress?

What may employees or employers do to clear up the situation when there is a controversy over which union, if any, is entitled to deal with an employer on behalf of his employees?

Before these and similar questions can be answered, it first is necessary to take a careful look at how the Taft-Hartley Act and the NLRB operate.

TWO TYPES OF LABOR LAWS

When it comes to enforcement, laws regulating labor-management relations are of two general kinds. One creates an agency to enforce the law. The Taft-Hartley Act belongs to this class. The other leaves it to the aggrieved party to bring action in the courts. The Railway Labor Act is an example of this type.

Under the Fair Labor Standards Act, both the Labor Department and aggrieved employees may bring court actions. Title VII of the Civil Rights Act also provides for suits both by the Equal Employment Opportunity Commission and by aggrieved individuals. The same is true under the Age Discrimination in Employment Act. But the government officials must attempt to resolve the dispute by conference, persuasion, and conciliation before authorizing a suit by an individual or a class action by a number of persons.

Sometimes agencies set up to enforce laws are known as quasi-judicial agencies—meaning that they are similar to courts in some respects. In other respects, they resemble the office of state attorney, being charged with the duty of prosecuting offenses on behalf of the government. So these agencies have two duties—(1) to prosecute violations, and (2) to judge whether a violation has occurred; and, if it has, to prescribe remedies.

SEPARATING PROSECUTOR FROM JUDGE

These two duties are present in all quasi-judicial agencies. In the case of the National Labor Relations Board, however, the two duties are separated more completely than in the case of any like body. The way this is done is rather complicated.

First, there is the Board itself. It consists of five members appointed by the President with the advice and consent of the Senate. It is essentially the judicial branch of the agency.

Second, there is the Board's General Counsel, also appointed by the President with the advice and consent of the Senate. The title is misleading because he does not advise the Board on points of law. This is done by the Solicitor of the Board. The General Counsel is the prosecutor. As such, he listens to charges that the law has been violated and determines which of the cases brought to him he should prosecute before the Board. If he decides not to prosecute a charge, it is virtually impossible to obtain review of his action. Once the Board has issued a decision, the General Counsel represents the Board in review or enforcement proceedings in the courts.

FACT-FINDING DUTIES

The NLRB and its General Counsel are more than an enforcement agency, however. They have fact-finding duties also. These include determining the bargaining agent employees in a bargaining unit wish to represent them and determining whether employees wish to get rid of a bargaining agent or a union-shop contract.

The General Counsel is entrusted by the Board with the duty of arranging for elections on these questions. The actual work is entrusted to the Board's regional offices, which the General Counsel supervises. The Board has delegated to its regional directors decision-making authority in election cases, subject to certain exceptions and possible review by the Board.

PROCEDURES ILLUSTRATED

It is possible to see how the Act operates in practice by taking two typical cases and following the steps as they take place. One case will arise from a charge of unfair labor practices; the other from a dispute as to bargaining agent. Although everything does not always happen the same way, the picture is roughly accurate.

Discharge of Employee—Suppose an employee who has just joined a union is discharged. He and the union officials may believe that the motive for his discharge was based on his having joined the union and that he is being made an example of as a means of discouraging others from joining. Acting through the union, he files a charge at the nearest regional office of the NLRB. Forms are provided for use in making the charge.

At this point, the employer first comes into contact with a Board agent, usually through a telephone call asking for an interview. One is arranged. It is possible the agent may be convinced that there has been a misunderstanding and that some other good reason existed for the discharge. But he will reach this conclusion only after he has satisfied himself by an investigation that it is true. He has authority to come into the plant, require access to records, and make whatever inquiries he may consider necessary.

The episode may end by dismissal of the charge by the regional director, although the union still may appeal to the General Counsel from the dismissal. But if the regional director believes that there is possible ground for the charge, the outcome will be different. In that case, the employer may decide to reinstate the employee. Otherwise, the regional director will issue a formal complaint against the employer charging him with violating the law.

(If the unfair-labor-practice charge is against a union and involves certain types of strikes, picketing, or boycotts, the General Counsel may be required to obtain an injunction against the conduct pending a decision by the Board in the case. See "Strikes, Picketing, Boycotts, and Lockouts" above. The General Counsel has discretion as to whether to seek an injunction in other types of unfair-labor-practice cases.)

In 1974, the NLRB and the bar in the New York City area began to experiment with pretrial discussions on cases to be tried before an administrative law judge. Previously pretrial discussions had been used in the San Francisco area on a motion basis. The objective was to produce more settlements or at least narrow the issues to be tried. About 85 percent of unfair-labor-practice charges filed with the Board are settled without a formal hearing.

THE FORMAL PROCEEDING

If settlement efforts fail, a formal proceeding begins. A hearing is arranged before an administrative law judge. The employer is confronted with the complaint and is given an opportunity to disprove the allegations, if possible. His adversary is an attorney from the office of the General Counsel, whose aim it is to convince the administrative law judge that the charges are supported by the facts. Witnesses testify and are cross-examined. Then the administrative law judge makes his decision.

Whatever the law judge's decision, each side may be given an opportunity to argue for or against it before the Board. The Board then makes its decision. The decision may be in the form of findings of fact, conclusions of law, and an order. The order may be a dismissal of the complaint. But more frequently it requires the employer to cease and desist from an unfair labor practice he is found to have committed. Additional orders, designed to undo the effects of the unfair practice, may be issued. These may include a requirement that the employer reinstate the employee with or without back pay. This ends the Board stage of the enforcement procedure.

Since the 1947 amendments to the Act, the Board also has policed unfair labor practices by unions. The 1959 Landrum-Griffin Act added to the restrictions. In the case of secondary boycotts and certain types of picketing, the Board is required to go to court and seek an injunction against the union's action.

ENFORCEMENT OF ORDER

A short period is allowed for compliance before the next stage is begun—appeal to the courts. The court proceeding may be initiated in two days. The Board may ask a federal court of appeals to enforce the order. Or the employer may ask the court to set the order aside.

If the court decides to enforce the order, then for the first time the employer feels the force of compulsion to comply. Failure to do so may bring contempt of court proceedings, with possible fine and imprisonment. There, of course, may be appeal to the Supreme Court of the United States.

When the courts are asked to enforce or set aside an order of the Board, the scales are weighted in favor of the Board. The Act requires the courts to accept the facts as found by the Board if they are supported by substantial evidence on the record considered as a whole. The Supreme Court, however, has said that this does not mean that the courts may not take into account contradictory evidence or evidence from which conflicting inferences could be drawn. The substantiality of evidence, it added, must take into account whatever in the record fairly detracts from its weight. (27 LRRM 2373)

Contempt Proceeding—A decree of a court enforcing an order of the Board is in effect a continuing injunction. Enforcement of the decree thus becomes the province of the court. This may be called the third stage of the enforcement of the law. It operates through the bringing of contempt proceedings by the Board.

This stage differs from earlier stages in that the court is its own fact finder. The court, moreover, may draw its own inferences from the facts and prescribe remedies without regard to the views of the Board.

REPRESENTATION DISPUTE

The second kind of dispute invokes the NLRB's fact-finding powers. It occurs when a union wants to be recognized as bargaining agent, but the employer wishes first to be assured that the union represents a majority of the employees in the appropriate unit. In such a case, the employer may wait for the union to take the initiative by filing a petition for certification or charges of refusal to bargain. But the employer also may take the initiative himself by filing a petition for an election with the Board.

Assuming that the employer takes the initiative, he obtains from the Board's regional office a form to make out, in which he enters information called for, including a statement that the union wishes to represent certain classifications of employees. After the regional office of the Board gets the form, it sends an official to look into the situation. If the official is satisfied that the employer's business affects interstate commerce and there is no obvious obstacle to an election, such as a valid contract with another union, he will call in the union and try to get an agreement between the employer and the union as to the unit of employees to be represented and as to other details.

If an agreement is reached, a consent election employing informal procedures will be conducted, the ballot providing for the choice of the union or for no union. If the union wins, it is declared bargaining agent and is certified as such.

If no agreement is reached between the union and employer, formal procedures are utilized. There is a hearing before a hearing officer, and findings are made as to the appropriate unit and whether to conduct an election. Even after the election has been held there may be challenges to ballots and election objections to be disposed of before any certification may be issued. The rules on these phases of the proceeding are discussed in detail earlier in the chapter on "Choosing a Bargaining Agent."

REVIEW OF DETERMINATIONS

Ordinarily determinations by the Board regarding bargaining units and bargaining agents are final, except as they may be reviewed in later refusal-to-bargain proceedings as arbitrary or lacking substantial evidence as a base. But the Supreme Court has held that the immunity from direct court review does not apply where the Board determination violates the terms of the Act itself, such as by including professional employees in a unit with non-professionals without the majority approval of the professionals (43 LRRM

2222). However, the Court held in 1964 that a federal district court could not enjoin an election directed by the Board notwithstanding the company's claim that it was not the employer of the employees involved (55 LRRM 2694).

JURISDICTIONAL DISPUTE PROCEEDINGS

With the objective of protecting employers against being caught in the middle of union disputes over job assignments, Section 8(b) (4) (D) of the Taft-Hartley Act made it an unfair labor practice for a union to attempt by picketing or striking to force an employer to assign work to one group of employees rather than to another. But Congress declined to rely solely on the machinery provided to remedy other unfair labor practices and added a unique preliminary step for the handling of Section 8(b) (4) (D) disputes. Section 10(k) provides that before passing on the unfair practice charge, the NLRB must first "determine the dispute" unless the parties have adjusted or agreed upon methods for voluntary adjustment of the dispute.

In making a "determination of the dispute," the Board for several years confined itself merely to determining whether the striking union was lawfully entitled to compel assignment of the work to its members by virtue of a contract or NLRB certification. It refrained from making an affirmative award of the disputed work. In 1961, however, the U.S. Supreme Court told the Board that its policy was not the correct one. The Court said that where two or more unions are claiming the right to perform work and the case is brought before the Board, it is the Board's duty to decide which group is right "and then specifically to award such tasks in accordance with its decision." The Board now makes such work-jurisdiction awards. (47 LRRM 2332, 49 LRRM 1684)

An unfair labor practice proceeding is instituted in these jurisdictional-strike cases where (1) private adjustment machinery exists but has broken down or (2) a Section 10(k) determination has been issued, but the parties have not complied with the finding. A ruling in the unfair practice proceeding is enforceable in the U.S. courts of appeals.

There are two other types of proceedings conducted by the Board—the decertification election and the union-shop deauthorization election. These are discussed in the chapters headed "Choosing a Bargaining Agent" and "Lawful and Unlawful Union Security Clauses."

RULE-MAKING PROCEEDING

Although the Board had been under pressure for several years to utilize its rule-making powers in establishing rules of general application, it did not invoke its rule-making powers until late 1970. The issue was the establishment of annual revenue standards for the assertion of jurisdiction over private universities and colleges. In establishing the standards, the Board followed the rules of the Administrative Procedure Act and held a formal hearing at which interested parties were permitted to present evidence. (75 LRRM 1442)

FREEDOM OF INFORMATION

As a result of the Freedom of Information Act, the NLRB has made a number of documents and reports available to the public. These include:

▶ The Classified Index of the NLRB and Related Court Decisions through February 1973. It may be purchased from the Government Printing Office.

▶ The Administrative Law Judges Manual. This also may be purchased from the GPO.

▶ General policy memoranda, such as that issued by the Board's General Counsel on the question of deferral to arbitration.

A revised Field Manual will be made available when completed, as also will be the Outline of Law and Procedure in Representation Cases and Hearing Officer's Guide.

EQUAL EMPLOYMENT OPPORTUNITY

Another vehicle for regulating employment and labor relations is Title VII of the Civil Rights Act of 1964, as amended by the Equal Employment Opportunity Act of 1972. An indication of its importance is the fact that the number of charges being filed under Title VII is more than double the number being filed under the Taft-Hartley Act.

The five-member Equal Employment Opportunity Commission is the principal agency policing employment discrimination by employers and employment agencies based on race, color, religion, sex, or national origin, and membership and hiring discrimination by unions on the same bases. In many cases, particularly where a collective bargaining contract is involved, the employees and the union may be joined as defendants in a Title VII action.

ADMINISTRATIVE STRUCTURE

There is a complicated administrative structure enforcing equal employment opportunity at the federal, state, and local levels. At the top of the structure is the EEOC. With the power given to it by the 1972 amendments to file actions in courts to enforce Title VII, it now is a full-fledged administrative and enforcement agency.

But this is only the tip of the iceberg. At the federal level, there are the Office of Federal Contract Compliance, which enforces Executive Order 11246, applicable to federal contractors, with the assistance of the procurement agencies; the Civil Service Commission, which enforces the program for federal employees under Executive Order 11478; the Justice Department, which enforces Title VII against state and local governments; the Labor Department's Employment Standards Administration, which enforces the Equal Pay Act and the Age Discrimination in Employment Act; the U.S. Civil Rights Commission; and the Department of Health, Education and Welfare in the medical-care area.

Then there are the state and local fair employment practices agencies. There are some 40 state boards or commissions and more than 70 local commissions. In a number of states that have no laws of statewide application, there are local human relations commissions. There are 32 states that, in addition to forbidding job discrimination based on the usual race, color, religion, sex, or national origin, also forbid discrimination based on age, while 18 forbid discrimination against the handicapped.

The EEOC may defer to these state and local agencies for 60 or 120 days, but it will defer only if the state or local law prohibits essentially the same practices barred by Title VII.

Under the Vocational Rehabilitation Act of 1973, discrimination against the handicapped is forbidden by federal law.

COVERAGE OF TITLE VII

The coverage of Title VII of the Civil Rights Act extends about as far as it is possible for Congress to reach under its authority to regulate interstate commerce.

An employer is a "person engaged in an industry affecting commerce," and a person is not only an individual of flesh and blood, but also comprehends the usual organizational structures that people establish to further a common purpose—labor unions, associations, corporations, mutual companies, joint-stock companies, trusts, and unincorporated associations. Legal representatives also are persons, and so are other people having certain legal responsibilities, such as trustees, trustees in bankruptcy, and receivers.

The 1972 amendments broadened the definition of "employer" to bring within the Act's coverage state and local governments, governmental agencies, political subdivisions, and departments and agencies of the District of Columbia, with certain narrow exceptions. The amendments also added a new section that makes clear the obligation of the Federal Government to make all personnel actions without discrimination based on race, color, sex, religion, or national origin. The authority to enforce equal employment opportunity in federal agencies is assigned to the Civil Service Commission.

There are two basic numbers that affect the standing of a "person" as an employer subject to Title VII:

▶ He must have 15 or more employees.

▶ He must have them for each working day in each of 20 or more calendar weeks in the current or preceding calendar year. Once these requirements are met, the employer is covered for two calendar years.

Practically everyone working for an enterprise is an "employee" for Title VII purposes. Although the definition of "employee" does not specifically cover job applicants, the 1972 amendments make it clear that it is unlawful for employers to discriminate against applicants for employment and for unions to discriminate against applicants for union membership.

RECRUITING, HIRING, PROMOTION

An essential ingredient to a nondiscriminatory employment policy is a basic procedure for recruiting and selecting employees that does not intentionally or inadvertently work to screen out minority group members. This is often the first place that federal officials look in judging whether a company is in compliance with the law. Similarly, a company must be able to show that it uses nondiscriminatory standards in promotion.

Determinations by the courts and the EEOC as to whether particular recruiting or promotion policies are racially discriminatory are usually based on the test laid down by the Supreme Court in Griggs v. Duke Power Co. (3 FEP Cases 175) The test is that, if an action or policy, although neutral on its face, is discriminatory in effect, it is unlawful unless it is shown that there is a substantial business justification for the policy.

Recruiting—Applying this test, the courts and the EEOC have found the following recruiting and hiring policies unlawful:

▶ A company's refusal to hire job applicants because of their arrest record. (5 FEP Cases 267)

▶ Word-of-mouth recruiting or recruiting only at predominantly white educational institutions, where there is an existing racial imbalance in the work force. (5 FEP Cases 587, 4 FEP Cases 313)

▶ A requirement that applicants have a high school education where there is no showing that the requirement is sufficiently related to job performance. (5 FEP Cases 587)

▶ Enforcement of grooming standards prohibiting "bush" hair styles or handlebar and Fu Manchu mustaches. (4 FEP Cases 840, 4 FEP Cases 18)

▶ Refusal to hire individuals because of their poor credit record. (4 FEP Cases 304)

▶ Rejection of applicants because of adverse personnel reports from other companies without giving them an opportunity to rebut the reports. (4 FEP Cases 1305, 1169)

▶ Preferential hiring of relatives of present employees where the existing workforce contains a disproportionately low percentage of minority workers. (3 FEP Cases 266)

▶ Denial of employment to unwed mothers in an area where blacks had a significantly higher rate of illegitimate births than whites and where there was no showing of business necessity. (3 FEP Cases 230)

Promotions—Policies for selecting employees for promotion generally must meet the same test set forth in the Duke and related decisions regarding policies for recruiting and hiring. Thus an appeals court held it unlawful for an employer to rely solely on the recommendations of foremen for transfer and promotion where it was shown that a disproportionately small percentage of black employees were upgraded or transferred and the standards used by the foremen were vague, subjective, and without any safeguards to ensure impartiality. (4 FEP Cases 445)

In promotions, as with hiring, the employer has the burden of proving an alleged business necessity for adhering to a challenged practice. It must be able to show not only a business purpose for the practice but also that it could not be replaced by another plan that would be just as efficacious for the business purpose but have a lesser racial impact. (6 FEP Cases 813)

EMPLOYMENT TESTING

The use of employment tests—defined by the EEOC as "any paper-and-pencil or performance measure used as a basis for any employment decision and all formal, scored, quantified or standardized techniques of assessing job suitability"—is the subject of considerable controversy in fair employment law. Title VII expressly provides that it is not unlawful for an employer to give and to act upon the results of any professionally developed ability or psychological test, provided that the test is not used to discriminate against women or minority group members.

This provision in Title VII is subject to two conflicting interpretations. Some say that it protects any test unless there is specific intent to use it for discriminatory purposes. The Supreme Court, however, has ruled that any test which has an adverse effect on women or minority group applicants must be validated as job related regardless of intent. (3 FEP Cases 175)

The EEOC has formulated testing guidelines "to serve as a workable set of standards for employers, unions and employment agencies in determining whether their selection procedures conform with the obligations contained in Title VII." Under the guidelines, tests which purport to measure applicants for relevant personal characteristics probably will almost never be deemed valid. Even a test that seems to measure job-related skills directly may not meet the guidelines. In order to ensure that even a job-related test meets the guidelines, the employer must conduct follow-up studies to demonstrate a correlation between test performance and job performance. Moreover, the test must be validated in this way for each minority group taking it, if this is technically feasible.

The most troublesome step in validating a test by measuring test performance against job performance is realistically measuring job performance. Though supervisors' ratings of employees may be helpful, the employer should look beyond such ratings. Where possible, work samples should be used. Above all, the employer must make sure that race and sex bias do not enter into the evaluation process.

EMPLOYMENT CONDITIONS

The federal policy against employment discrimination based on race, color, religion, sex, or national origin extends to virtually every aspect of the employer-employee relationship. The following rundown of EEOC decisions illustrates the variety of ways in which disparate treatment based on race or national origin can be found. Violations were found where:

▶ Caucasian employees averaged higher Christmas bonuses than black employees, and the employer's stated reason failed to withstand scrutiny. (EEOC Sixth Annual Report)

▶ Safety rules were applied disparately, and it was shown that race was a factor in the administration of the rules. (3 FEP Cases 1025)

▶ Crews were either all-white or all-black, with no evidence to show the basis for crew assignments, and the white crews enjoyed better housing than the blacks. (3 FEP Cases 384)

▶ A racially prejudiced supervisor was retained, affecting not only the terms and conditions of present employees but also the potential hiring of new black employees. (EEOC Sixth Annual Report)

▶ The use of Spanish during working as well as nonworking time was banned, where there was no showing of a need for supervisors to understand all conversations among the Spanish-surnamed employees. (EEOC Sixth Annual Report)

▶ A black employee was discharged for a physical assault on his foreman after being subjected to prolonged racial intimidation and harassment by the foreman. (3 FEP Cases 142)

▶ A working atmosphere was maintained in which racial insults were permitted. (EEOC Sixth Annual Report)

► A white employee was discharged because she befriended blacks. (3 FEP Cases 1244)

► Standards of employee appearance and grooming were enforced "without regard to their racially different physiological and cultural characteristics." (4 FEP Cases 16)

SENIORITY, REFERRAL SYSTEMS

Title VII prohibits segregation by race, religion, sex, or national origin in collective bargaining units, lines of promotion, seniority groups, and the like. An exception permits discrimination that is based on a "bona fide" seniority system, so long as the system isn't a guise for unlawful discrimination.

The key issue that has arisen regarding seniority is the impact of Title VII on seniority systems that had discriminated against minority groups prior to the passage of Title VII but were changed to employ "neutral" criteria from that point on. The question raised can be variously stated as—

► Can Title VII weaken or destroy the current and future seniority rights of white workers because such rights were earned under a formerly discriminatory seniority system?

► Can blacks be permanently locked into inferior positions because of seniority rights earned under a formerly discriminatory system?

Similar questions have been raised regarding job referral systems of unions that formerly were all-white.

Seniority systems—In deciding cases raising the question of Title VII's impact on seniority systems that were formerly discriminatory but were changed to employ "neutral" criteria, the courts have considered three different approaches. Under one approach—"freedom now"—black workers would replace white incumbents who hold jobs that, but for past discrimination under the seniority system, blacks might hold. Under a second approach—"status quo"—employers could use the seniority system for all the purposes set out for it in the collective bargaining agreement, without worrying about the unfortunate effects on the future job bidding of blacks who failed to accumulate seniority because they were victims of past discrimination.

Finally, under the "rightful place" approach, Title VII would be construed as prohibiting the future awarding of vacant jobs on the basis of seniority systems that reflect past discrimination. No white incumbents would be replaced by blacks, but employers would have to take steps to prevent adverse effects on the future bidding of blacks victimized by past discrimination.

The "rightful place" approach has been adopted by the majority of courts evaluating seniority systems in light of Title VII. These courts have reasoned that the "freedom now" approach is unacceptable because it results in preferential treatment for blacks, while the "status quo" approach is unacceptable because it perpetuates past discrimination. Only the "rightful place" approach, it is argued, prevents the carrying forward of past discrimination without granting preferential treatment to any racial group. (1 FEP Cases 875, 2 FEP Cases 426, 3 FEP Cases 653, 1 FEP Cases 260)

Once a court decides that future job openings will be awarded to blacks who would have the requisite seniority but for past discrimination, it must further determine the pay rate and seniority status to which the black worker is entitled. The problem arises where the employer has maintained separate job classifications for whites and blacks. Though the "white" jobs may be more desirable than the "black" jobs, other things being equal, if the black worker who transfers to the formerly white job must begin the new job at entry level, he may be faced with the prospect of loss of seniority and a pay reduction. The courts have recognized, however, that adjustments in the system may be necessary to prevent such consequences. (1 FEP Cases 875, 3 FEP Cases 653, 6 FEP Cases 677)

Union referral systems—Seemingly "neutral" criteria for job referrals from a union hiring hall may encounter difficulties when examined by courts adopting the rightful-place doctrine. In cases where unions with histories of excluding blacks began to admit blacks but continued to use longstanding referral rules granting work priority to those with work experience which the blacks could not gain because of their exclusion from the union, the courts have said that the union referral rules are incompatible with Title VII. (1 FEP Cases 387, 2 FEP Cases 127) Referral rules based on nepotism have received the same treatment. (1 FEP Cases 577)

Layoffs—A particularly difficult issue is presented when a company that discriminated in the past must lay-off workers. The most common procedure used by companies in this position is to lay off the least senior workers. In the only appeals court ruling on the layoff issue in the Title VII context, the Seventh Circuit decided that a company that used the "last hired, first fired" principle to determine layoff policy did not violate Title VII or the Civil Rights Act of 1866. It reasoned that a layoff policy based on a company-wide seniority system does not perpetuate past discrimination. Only when black workers have been restricted in their ability to transfer and gain promotions under department seniority systems would use of the seniority system perpetuate discrimination, the court said. (8 FEP Cases 577)

Several district courts, however, have ruled that a layoff policy based on seniority violates Title VII if, because of past discrimination, blacks were unable to accumulate the relevant seniority, be it company wide or department wide. (7 FEP Cases 90, 8 FEP Cases 690, 959)

SEX DISCRIMINATION

Title VII of the Civil Rights Act was drafted primarily to deal with discrimination based on race, national origin, and religion. The ban on sex discrimination was inserted during the congressional debate with little accompanying discussion to clarify the legislative intent. It is not surprising, therefore, that the EEOC has had more difficulty clarifying and applying the ban on sex discrimination than any other single provision of the law. Moreover, it has had to relate the ban on sex discrimination in Title VII with the overlapping provisions of the Equal Pay Act when dealing with charges of wage discrimination.

EEOC Guidelines—Guidelines published by the EEOC in 1972 make the following major points:

▶ It is unlawful employment practice to classify a job as "male" or "female" or to maintain separate lines of progression or separate seniority lists based on sex, where this would adversely affect any employee, unless sex is a bona fide occupational qualification for that job.

▶ Advertising in "male" and "female" help-wanted columns is unlawful, unless sex is bona fide occupational qualification.

▶ State "protective" laws for women—laws that limit the employment of females in certain occupations, in jobs requiring the lifting or carrying of weights exceeding certain prescribed limits, during certain hours of the night, for more than a specified number of hours per day or per week, or for certain periods of time before and after childbirth—conflict with and are superseded by Title VII. Accordingly, such laws will not be considered a defense to an otherwise established unlawful employment practice or as a basis for the application of the bona fide occupational qualification exception. The majority of states, however, still have so-called "protective" laws.

▶ Rules that limit or restrict the employment of married women and are not applicable to married men constitute discrimination based on sex.

▶ An employer may not discriminate between men and women with regard to "fringe benefits," including medical, hospital, accident, life insurance and retirement benefits, profit-sharing, and bonus plans, EEOC has ruled. Additionally, conditioning the benefits available to employees and their spouses on whether the employee is the "head of the household" or "principal wage earner" will be found a prima facie violation of the prohibitions against sex discrimination contained in Title VII, since such status bears no relationship to job performance.

▶ It is unlawful for an employer to make available benefits for the wives and families of male employees where the same benefits are not made available for husbands and families of female employees; it also is unlawful to make available benefits for the wives of male employees that are not made available to female employees, or to make available benefits for the husbands of female employees that are not available to male employees.

▶ An employment policy that excludes from employment applicants or employees because of pregnancy is in prima facie violation of Title VII.

Bona fide occupational qualification—The ban on discrimination based on religion, sex, or national origin makes an exception for discrimination that involves a bona fide occupational qualification. The EEOC has said the exception to the general ban on sex discrimination should be construed narrowly. It would not apply in these situations, for example:

▶ A refusal to hire a woman based on assumptions of the comparative employment characteristics of women, such as the assumption that women have a higher turnover rate than men.

▶ A refusal to hire based on stereotyped characterizations of sexes, e.g., that men are less capable of assembling intricate equipment or women are less capable of aggressive salesmanship.

▶ A refusal to hire because of the preferences of coworkers, the employer, clients, or customers (except where it is necessary for the purposes of authenticity or genuineness, such as the preference for actresses to play female parts).

The courts generally have construed the BFOQ exception narrowly, although perhaps not so narrowly as EEOC. Leading interpretations include the following:

► In a case involving a company rule against hiring women with preschool age children, the Supreme Court said that the test of whether a bona fide occupational qualification exists is whether it can be shown that the qualification is "demonstrably more relevant to job performance for a woman than a man." (3 FEP Cases 40)

► In a case involving the refusal to employ women as telephone "switchmen" because of asserted "strenuous" lifting involved, an appeals court said the test of whether a BFOQ exists is whether there is "reasonable cause to believe, that is, a factual basis for believing, that all or substantially all women would be unable to perform safely and efficiently the duties of the job involved." (1 FEP Cases 656)

► In rejecting the argument that sex (female) is a BFOQ for a flight cabin attendant, an appeals court said the test is whether "the essence of the business operation would be undermined by not hiring members of one sex exclusively." (3 FEP Cases 337)

► In finding no BFOQ in a rule requiring stewardesses (but not stewards) to be unmarried, an appeals court said: "The marital status of a stewardess cannot be said to affect the individual woman's ability to create the proper psychological climate of comfort, safety, and security for passengers. Nor does any passenger preference for single stewardesses provide a valid reason for invoking the rule." (3 FEP Cases 621)

Maternity benefits and leave—The Supreme Court has held that California's policy of not providing insurance under its disability benefits program for women unable to work because of normal pregnancy does not violate the Equal Protection Clause of the Constitution. (8 FEP Cases 97) The Court did not decide whether an insurance program like California's, or any other scheme that denies compensation for losses due to pregnancy, would violate Title VII. It has said, however, that EEOC guidelines are entitled to "great deference" whenever a Title VII issue is raised. On the issue of pregnancy, EEOC guidelines provide that inability to work caused by pregnancy or childbirth is a disability just like any other and should be treated as such in situations involving commencement and duration of leave, accrual of seniority, reinstatement, and payment under insurance or sick leave plans. The guidelines specifically state that any insurance plan that provides nonoccupational sickness and accident benefits for employees, but excludes disabilities due to pregnancy, discriminates because of sex and thus violates Title VII.

District courts have split on the question of how the EEOC guidelines on pregnancy should be treated. Two such courts ruled that refusal to pay sickness and accident benefits for pregnancy-related disabilities was a violation of Title VII. (7 FEP Cases 796, 271) Two others reached the opposite conclusion. (7 FEP Cases 26, 8 FEP Cases 529)

As to maternity leave, the Supreme Court has ruled that mandatory leave provisions requiring a pregnant teacher to leave her job four or five months before childbirth are in violation of the Due Process Clause of the Constitution. (6 FEP Cases 1253)

RELIGIOUS DISCRIMINATION

Cases involving religious discrimination handled by the EEOC have been considerably fewer in number than cases of race, sex, or national origin. Similarly, there have been relatively few legal interpretations and court decisions on the subject. However, the EEOC has issued guidelines on religious discrimination for employers which stress the following points:

▶ Under Title VII requirements, an employer has the obligation to make "reasonable accommodation" to the religious needs of his employees, where such accommodation does not impose undue hardship on the employer.

▶ It is up to the employer to prove that making such accommodation would cause undue hardship in a particular case.

▶ Because of the "varied religious practices of the American people," the Commission will consider each case of religious discrimination on an individual basis.

In the leading case of Dewey v. Reynolds Metal Co., the Sixth Circuit ruled that it was a "reasonable accommodation" for an employer to insist that an employee work on Sunday, even though it was contrary to his religious beliefs, or obtain a replacement. (2 FEP Cases 687) The ruling was affirmed by an equally divided Supreme Court. (3 FEP Cases 508)

The 1972 amendments to Title VII provided statutory authorization for the positions taken by the EEOC in its guidelines. Since the adoption of the amendments, appeals courts have found violations where employers took adverse action against Seventh Day Adventists because of their refusal to work on their Saturday sabbath. (4 FEP Cases 951, 5 FEP Cases 69)

NATIONAL ORIGIN DISCRIMINATION

Although the term "national origin" is not defined in Title VII or other federal statutes relating to job discrimination, it has come to mean the country of one's ancestry, rather than race or color. The majority of national origin discrimination cases thus far have involved Spanish-surname Americans—a group including Mexican Americans, Puerto Ricans, and others of Spanish heritage.

The Commission has made the following points in its guidelines regarding discrimination on the basis of national origin:

▶ Although Title VII provides for a BFOQ (bona fide occupational qualification) exception for national origin cases, this exception will be "strictly construed."

▶ The EEOC will examine "with particular concern" cases involving national origin discrimination of a covert nature—that is, where an individual is discriminated against because of a character peculiar to his heritage.

▶ Discrimination against a lawfully domiciled alien amounts to discrimination for citizenship and hence for national origin. However, the Supreme Court ruled in the Espinoza case that aliens are not protected by Title VII and, on this reasoning, upheld a company's longstanding policy of not hiring aliens. (6 FEP Cases 933) But in a case brought under the 1866 Act, a court held that an employer violated the Act by refusing to hire a person because he was not a citizen. (8 FEP Cases 433) Moreover, the Supreme Court held that the Equal Protection Clause barred a state from excluding an alien from the state's competitive civil service. (5 FEP Cases 1152) This principle subsequently was extended by an appeals court to hold unconstitutional the U.S. Civil Service Commission's regulation forbidding the employment of aliens. (7 FEP Cases 58)

▶ State and local laws prohibiting the employment of noncitizens are in conflict with and are therefore superseded by Title VII.

DISCRIMINATION BY UNIONS

Where a union acts as an employer, it must not violate any of the prohibitions imposed on employers generally. In its capacity as a union, a union may not do any of the following:

▶ Exclude or expel from membership or otherwise discriminate against an individual because of his race, color, religion, sex, national origin, or age.

▶ Limit, segregate, or classify members and applicants for membership or fail or refuse to refer an individual for employment in any way that would deprive or tend to deprive him of employment opportunities or would limit such opportunities or otherwise adversely affect his status as an employee or as an applicant for employment because of his race, color, religion, sex, national origin, or age.

▶ Cause or attempt to cause an employer to discriminate against an individual because of his race, color, religion, sex, national origin, or age.

▶ Operate or join with employers in the operation of an apprenticeship training or retraining program in which discrimination is practiced on the basis of race, color, religion, sex, or national origin.

GLOSSARY OF LABOR TERMS

The current language of labor relations in the United States reflects the later steps of a transitional stage.

Many of the words used in describing events arising from the employer-employee relationship took on their present meaning in an environment of conflict, often breaking out into a form of private warfare.

The newer words are mainly those closely associated with the language of laws and governmental agencies. They bear witness to an increasing element of governmental regulation to replace the more or less open hostility of earlier days.

The definitions which follow are intended as a guide in the understanding of talk or writing on industrial relations.

Many of the words have generally understood meanings outside of their usage in the labor field. In this glossary, however, only those meanings are given which are peculiar to their usage in labor relations.

Administrative law judge—Official who conducts hearings and makes recommendations to the NLRB or other government agency. (Formerly called a trial or hearing examiner.)

Affecting commerce—Test of application of the Taft-Hartley Act. If a business is such that a labor dispute would threaten interruption of or burden interstate commerce, the jurisdiction of the National Labor Relations Board comes into play.

Affirmative order—Command issued by a labor relations board requiring the persons found to have engaged in unfair labor practices to take such steps as will, so far as possible, undo the effect of such practices.

Agency shop — A contract requiring nonmembers of the contracting union to pay to the union or a designated charity a sum equal to union dues.

Agent—Person acting for an employer or a union; act of the agent implicates the principal for whom the agent acts in the matter of unfair labor practices or of conduct subject to court action whether or not specifically authorized or approved.

Agent provocateur—Person hired to provoke industrial strife for the purpose of weakening a union.

All-union shop—A term sometimes applied to arrangement more specifically described by the terms closed shop or union shop. See *Closed Shop, Union Shop.*

Annual improvement factor—Annual wage increase, fixed in advance as to amount, and granted on the premise that the employees are entitled to share in the long-term increase in the productivity of a company or industry.

Annual wage — Wages paid under terms that guarantee a specified minimum for the year or a minimum period of employment for the year.

Anticertification strike—Strike designed to force an employer to cease recognizing a union which has been certified as bargaining agent and to recognize the striking union instead. This is an unfair labor practice under the Taft-Hartley Act as to which a court injunction must be asked if it is believed that a complaint should be issued.

Anti-Closed-Shop Laws — See *Right to work.*

Anti-Injunction Acts—Federal and state statutes that limit the jurisdiction of courts to issue injunctions in labor disputes. See *Injunction.*

Antitrust Laws—Federal and state statutes to protect trade and commerce from unlawful restraints and monopolies. For many years, they were used to restrict union activities such as strikes, picketing, and boycotts. In recent years, however, their use in labor cases has been limited by statute and judicial interpretation.

Appropriate unit—See *Unit.*

Arbitration—Method of deciding a controversy under which parties to the controversy have agreed in advance to accept the award of a third party.

Authorization card — Statement signed by employee designating a union as authorized to act as his agent in collective bargaining.

Automation—Term used by industrial engineers to describe mechanical materials handling and the new computer technology that can automate entire factories. It sometimes is used loosely to describe any technological improvement.

Back pay—Wages required to be paid to employees who have been discharged in violation of a legal right, either one based on a law or acquired by contract.

Back-to-work movement—Organized effort to reopen a struck plant, participated in by employees opposed to the strike and by the business community, sometimes with police aid.

Bargaining unit — See *Unit.*

Blacklist—List of names of persons or firms to be discriminated against, either in the matter of employment or patronage. See *Unfair list.*

Board of inquiry—Body to be appointed by President to mediate and report in national-emergency disputes under the Taft-Hartley Act.

Bona fide union—A union chosen or organized freely by employees without unlawful influence on the part of their employer.

Bureau of Labor Statistics—Bureau in the Labor Department that issues statistics affecting labor relations, including the Consumer Price Index to which some wage adjustments are tied.

Bootleg contract—A collective bargaining agreement which is contrary to the policy of the Taft-Hartley Act, such as a closed shop. Enforcement of such contracts may eventually entail back-pay awards, but this risk is sometimes considered outweighed by the advantages of avoiding a strike.

Boycott—Refusal to deal with or buy the products of a business as a means of exerting pressure in a labor dispute.

Business agent—Paid representative of a local union who handles its grievance actions and negotiates with employers, enrolling of new members, and other membership and general business affairs. Sometimes called a walking delegate.

Captive audience — Employees required to attend a meeting in which an employer makes an anti-union speech shortly before an election. Now an employer need give the union an opportunity to answer such a speech under similar conditions only if he enforces a broad no-solicitation rule.

Card check—Checking union authorization cards signed by employees against employer's payroll to determine whether union represents a majority of the employer's employees.

Casual workers—Persons irregularly employed.

Cease-and-desist order — Command issued by a labor relations board requiring employer or union to abstain from unfair labor practice.

Central labor union—Federation of union locals in one city or county having affiliations with different national unions but same parent body.

Certification — Official designation by a labor board of a labor organization entitled to bargain as exclusive representative of employees in a certain unit. See *Unit.*

Charge—Formal allegations against employer or union under labor relations acts on the basis of which, if substantiated, a complaint may be issued by the board or commission.

Checkoff—Arrangement under which an employer deducts from pay of employees the amount of union dues and turns over the proceeds to the treasurer of the union.

Closed shop—Arrangement between an employer and a union under which only members of the union may be hired. See *Union shop.*

Coalition (Coordinated) bargaining—Joint or cooperative efforts by a group of unions in negotiating contracts with an employer who deals with a number of unions.

Coercion—Economic or other pressure exerted by an employer to prevent the free exercise by employees of their right to self-organization and collective bargaining; intimidation by union or fellow employees to compel affiliation with union.

Collective bargaining—Negotiations looking toward a labor contract between an organization of employees and their employer or employers.

Collective bargaining contract—Formal agreement over wages, hours, and conditions of employment entered into between an employer or group of employers and one or more unions representing employees of the employers.

Company police—Deputized police

officers paid by an employer to protect his premises but used also at times to combat strikers or pickets.

Company town–Towns in which the land and houses are owned by a company which is the sole or chief employer in the town.

Company union–Organizations of employees of a single employer usually with implication of employer domination.

Concerted activities–Activities undertaken jointly by employees for the purpose of union organization, collective bargaining, or other mutual aid or protection. Such activities are "protected" under the Taft-Hartley Act.

Conciliation–Efforts by third party toward the accommodation of opposing viewpoints in a labor dispute so as to effect a voluntary settlement.

Consent decree–Court order entered with the consent of the parties.

Consent election–Election held by a labor board after informal hearing in which various parties agree on terms under which the election is to be held.

Constructive discharge–Unfavorable treatment of employee marked for discharge so that employee will "voluntarily" resign.

Consumer picketing–Picketing of a retail store in which the pickets urge customers not to patronize the store or to buy a particular product. If the picketing is in support of a strike against a producer or supplier, the picketing is legal if it is aimed merely at getting customers not to buy products of the struck employer. It is unlawful if it is aimed at getting the customers to stop patronizing the store entirely.

Consumer Price Index–An index prepared monthly by the Labor Department's Bureau of Labor Statistics measuring changes in prices of a specific "market basket" of commodities and services. It is significant in labor relations because wage escalation under some collective bargaining contracts is tied to the index.

Contract-bar rules–Rules applied by the NLRB in determining when an existing contract between an employer and a union will bar a representation election sought by a rival union.

Contracting out–See *Subcontracting.*

Cooling-off period–Period during which employees are forbidden to strike under laws which require a definite period of notice before a walkout.

Craft union–Labor organization admitting to membership persons engaged in a specified type of work, usually involving a special skill.

Craft unit–Bargaining unit consisting of workers following a particular craft or using a particular type of skill, such as molders, carpenters, etc.

Damage suits–Suits which may be brought in federal courts, without the usual limitations, to recover damages for breach of collective bargaining contracts and for violation of prohibitions against secondary boycotts and other unlawful strike action under the Taft-Hartley Act.

Deauthorization election – Election held by the NLRB under the Taft-Hartley Act to determine whether employees wish to deprive their union bargaining agent of authority to bind them under a union-shop contract.

Decertification—Withdrawal of bargaining agency from union upon vote by employees in unit that they no longer wish to be represented by union.

Discharge—Permanent separation of employee from payroll by employer.

Discrimination—Short form for "discrimination in regard to hire or tenure of employment as a means of encouraging or discouraging membership in a labor organization;" also refusal to hire, promote, or admit to union membership because of race, creed, color, sex, or national origin.

Discriminatory discharge—Discharge for union activity, or because of race, color, religion, sex, or national origin.

Domination—Control exercised by an employer over a union of his employees.

Dual union — Labor organization formed to enlist members among workers already claimed by another union.

Economic strike—Strike not caused by unfair labor practice of an employer.

Election—See *Employee election.*

Emergency board—Body appointed under Railway Labor Act by President of the United States when a strike or lockout is imminent on interstate railroads. See *Board of inquiry.*

Emergency dispute—A labor dispute in which a strike would imperil the national health and safety. Special procedures are provided under the Taft-Hartley Act for dealing with such disputes.

Employee association—Term sometimes used for plant union.

Employee election—Balloting by employees for the purpose of choosing a bargaining agent or unseating one previously recognized. See *Referendum.*

Employee representation plan—System under which employees select representatives to a joint body on which the management is also represented, the purpose of the body being to discuss grievances or company policy.

Employer association — Organization of employers in related enterprises, usually acting together in labor policy or bargaining as a unit with one or more unions.

Employer unit—Bargaining unit consisting of all production and maintenance employees working for one employer.

Employment contract — Agreement entered into between an employer and one or more employees. See *Collective bargaining contract, Individual contract.*

Equal Employment Opportunity Act of 1972—Act giving Equal Employment Opportunity Commission authority to sue in federal courts where it finds reasonable cause to believe that there has been employment discrimination based on race, color, religion, sex, or national origin.

Escalator clause—Clause in collective bargaining contract requiring wage or salary adjustments at stated intervals in a ratio to changes in the Consumer Price Index.

Escape period—A period, normally

15 days, during which employees may resign from a union so as not to be bound to continue membership under membership-maintenance agreements.

Espionage—Practice of spying on employees with a view to discovering membership in, or activity for, labor organizations.

Exactions—Payment under more or less direct duress for work not done and not intended to be done. Under the Taft-Hartley Act, seeking exactions is an unfair labor practice and making or receiving such payments is a crime for employers and unions or individuals.

Extortionate picketing—Picketing for the personal profit or enrichment of an individual, except through a bona fide increase in wages or other employee benefits, by taking or obtaining any money or other thing of value from the employer against his will or with his consent. Such picketing was made a federal crime by the Labor-Management Reporting and Disclosure Act.

Fact-finding boards — Agencies appointed, usually by a government official, to determine facts and make recommendations in major disputes. See *Board of inquiry*.

Fair employment practice—Term applied in some statutes to conduct which does not contravene prohibitions against discrimination in employment because of race, color, religion, sex, or national origin.

Featherbedding—Contractual requirements that employees be hired in jobs for which their services are not needed. See *Exactions*.

Fink—One who makes a career of taking employment in struck plants or of acting as a strike breaker, strike guard, or slugger.

Free riders — A term sometimes applied by unions to nonmembers within the unit represented by the union, the implication being that they obtain without cost the benefits of a contract obtained through the efforts of the dues-paying members.

Free speech—The right of employers to express views hostile to unionization, provided no threat of coercion or promise of benefit is contained therein. If the expression of views is coercive, it becomes unlawful interference with employees' rights.

Freeze Order—Government order freezing wages, salaries, prices, and rents as of a particular date, such as issued during the Korean War and in August 1971.

Fringe benefits — Term used to encompass items such as vacations, holidays, insurance, medical benefits, pensions, and other similar benefits that are given to an employee under his employment or union contract in addition to direct wages.

Furlough—Period of layoff.

General Counsel—Officer of the National Labor Relations Board whose chief duty is to issue and prosecute complaints in unfair labor practice cases presented to the Board for decision.

Good-faith bargaining—The type of bargaining an employer and a majority union must engage in to meet their bargaining obligation under the Taft-Hartley Act. The parties are required to meet at reasonable times and to confer in good faith with respect to wages, hours, and other terms and conditions of employment. But neither party is required to agree to a proposal or to make a concession.

Goon—Plugugly employed in labor dispute for the purpose of using or resisting violence.

Gorilla—Physically powerful person employed in labor disputes where violence is intended or expected.

Grievance—An employee complaint; an allegation by an employee, union, or employer that a collective bargaining contract has been violated.

Grievance committee – Committee designated by a union to meet periodically with the management to discuss grievances that have accumulated.

Guard—Plant protection employee. May not be represented by union affiliated with union of production employees under Taft-Hartley Act.

Hiring hall—Place where workers are recruited for ships or waterfront activities or for work on construction projects.

Homework—Piecework performed by workers in their own homes.

Hooking—Entrapping an employee into spying on fellow employees. Usually accomplished by approaching the prospective hooked man under a pretext and engaging him to write reports.

Hot goods – Term applied by union members to products of plants employing strikebreakers, nonunion workers, or other workers regarded as hostile by union. Hot-goods or hot-cargo clauses under which a union gets an employer to agree not to require his employees to handle or work on hot goods or cargo were outlawed by one of the 1959 amendments to the Taft-Hartley Act.

Immunity clause—Clause in a contract designed to protect a union from suits for contract violation growing out of unauthorized strikes. A typical clause would limit recourse of the parties to the grievance procedure of the contract.

Impartial umpire—Person designated by agreement between a union and an employer or association of employers whose duty it is to arbitrate grievances or controversies arising under a contract.

Independent union—Local labor organization not affiliated with a national organized union; union not affiliated with a national federation of unions.

Individual contract – Agreement of employer with individual employee covering conditions of work.

Industrial union—Labor organization admitting to membership all persons employed in a plant or industry, regardless of kind of work performed.

Industrial union council—Term used by CIO as equivalent to AFL term central labor union. See *Central labor union.*

Industrial unit – Bargaining unit composed of all production and maintenance workers in one or more plants, irrespective of the type of work done.

Informational picketing – Picketing for the purpose of advising the public, including other union members, that the picketed employer does not have a union contract or is selling goods produced by a struck or nonunion employer. The 1959 amendments to the Taft-Hartley Act placed restrictions on such picketing.

Initiation fees – Fees required by unions as a condition to the privilege of becoming members. If such fees are excessive or discriminatory, an employer may not be held to the obligation under a union shop of discharging employees who do not join the union.

Injunction–Mandatory order by a court to perform or cease a specified activity usually on the ground that otherwise the complaining party will suffer irreparable injury from unlawful actions of the other party.

Inside man–Spy placed in a plant as an employee.

Inside union–Plant union without outside affiliation.

Inspector–Euphemism used to refer to spies in accounts, correspondence, etc.

Interference–Short-cut expression for "interference with the right of employees to self-organization and to bargain collectively."

International union – Nationally organized union having locals in another country, usually Canada.

Intimidation–Actual or implied threats to induce employees to refrain from joining or to join a labor organization; threats used in other aspects of labor controversies, such as in picketing.

Joint council–Body established in some industries consisting of representatives of union and of employer association, its purposes being the settlement of disputes arising under a contract; body representing several craft unions in a plant or plants acting as a unit in collective bargaining.

Judicial review–Proceedings before courts for enforcement or setting aside of orders of labor relations boards. Review is limited to conclusions of law, excluding findings of fact unless these are unsupported by evidence.

Jurisdiction–Right claimed by union to organize class of employees without competition from any other union; province within which any agency or court is authorized to act. See *Work jurisdiction.*

Jurisdictional dispute – Controversy between two unions over the right to organize a given class or group of employees or to have members employed on a specific type of work.

Jurisdictional strike–A strike called to compel an employer to assign work to one class or craft of employees rather than to another. This is an unfair labor practice under the Taft-Hartley Act and may bring the question as to proper work assignment to the Labor Board for final decision.

Kickback – Return of a portion of wages paid, usually in pursuance of an undisclosed agreement with the person who hires the employee.

Labor contract–Agreement entered into between an employer and an organization of his employees covering wages, hours, and conditions of labor.

Labor dispute–As used in Norris-La-Guardia Act, a controversy involving persons in the same occupations or having interest therein or who work for the same employer or employers or who are members of the same or an affiliated union.

Labor Management Relations Act, 1947 – Basic law regulating labor relations of firms whose business affects interstate commerce. It became law over the President's veto on June 23, 1947.

Labor-Management Reporting and Disclosure Act—Statute adopted in 1959 that established code of conduct for unions, union officers, employers, and labor relations consultants. It also made some significant amendments to the Taft-Hartley Act. Also popularly known as Landrum-Griffin Act.

Labor relations board—Quasi-judicial agency set up under National or State Labor Relations Acts whose duty it is to issue and adjudicate complaints alleging unfair labor practices; to require such practices to be stopped; and to certify bargaining agents for employees.

Layoff—Dropping a worker temporarily from the pay roll, usually during a period of slack work, the intention being to rehire him when he is needed.

Local—Group of organized employees holding a charter from a national or international labor organization. A local is usually confined to union members in one plant or one small locality.

Lockout—Closing down of a business as a form of economic pressure upon employees to enforce acceptance of employer's terms, or to prevent whipsawing where union bargains with an association of employers.

Lodge—Term used in some labor organizations as the equivalent of Local. See *Local.*

Loyal worker—Employee who refuses to join outside labor organization or to participate in strike. Term used by employer.

Maintenance of membership—Union-security agreement under which employees who are members of a union on specified date, or thereafter become members, are required to remain members during the term of the contract as a condition of employment.

Majority rule—Rule that the representative chosen by the majority of employees in an appropriate unit shall be the exclusive bargaining agent for all the employees.

Make-whole order—Order issued by the NLRB requiring an employer who has refused to bargain in good faith under the Taft-Hartley Act to reimburse the employees for increased wages and other benefits they would have obtained had the employer bargained in good faith. The legality of such an order is in dispute.

Management-rights clause—Collective bargaining contract clause that expressly reserves to management certain rights and specifies that the exercise of those rights shall not be subject to the grievance procedure or arbitration.

Mandatory injunction—Term applied to injunctions that the NLRB General Counsel is required to seek in the case of alleged unfair practices involving secondary boycotts, secondary-recognition strikes, recognition or organizational picketing, or strikes to force an employer to ignore an NLRB certification. Injunction remains in effect pending decision by the NLRB on the merits of the case.

Mediation—Offer of good offices to parties to a dispute as an equal friend of each; differs from conciliation in that mediator makes proposals for settlement of the dispute that have not been made by either party.

Mediation Service—Short form for Federal Mediation and Conciliation Service, which has a functional part in settlement of disputes under the Taft-Hartley Act.

Membership maintenance – Requirement under which employees who are members of the contracting union or who become so must remain members during the life of the contract as a condition of employment.

Militarized guard—Plant guard under authority of armed services in factories where work is being done under contract with armed services. Militarized guards are on payroll of factory.

Missionary—Spy whose chief work is to spread antiunion or antistrike propaganda in the general neighborhood of a plant and particularly among the wives of workers. Usually not employed in the plant.

Mohawk Valley Formula—Strategy of strike-breaking involving a combination of direct methods with organizing of antiunion sentiment and devices for undermining the morale of strikers. (1-A LRR Man. 4)

Moonlighting – Practice of holding down two or more jobs at once, the second one usually being on a night shift: The Bureau of Labor Statistics estimates that 10 percent of the work force engages in this practice.

Multiple employer unit – Bargaining unit consisting of all production and maintenance workers employed by more than one employer.

Multiple plant unit—Bargaining unit consisting of all production and maintenance workers in two or more plants among a larger number owned by one employer.

National Labor Relations Act—Act passed July 5, 1935, known popularly as Wagner Act; amended form of the same incorporated as Title I of the Labor Management Relations Act, 1947, which became law June 23, 1947; also amended by Title VII of the Landrum-Griffin Act in 1959.

National Mediation Board—Agency set up under the Railway Labor Act to mediate in case of labor disputes in railroad and air transport industry and to conduct elections for choice of bargaining agents.

National Railroad Adjustment Board—Agency set up under the Railway Labor Act to settle disputes in railroad industry arising out of grievances or application of contracts.

Negotiating committee – Committee of a union or an employer selected to negotiate a collective bargaining contract.

Norris-LaGuardia Act – Popular name for Federal Anti-Injunction Act, approved Mar. 23, 1932.

Occupational Safety and Health Act—Law adopted in 1970 giving the Federal Government authority to prescribe and enforce safety and health standards in most industries.

Open Shop—Plant where employees are declared by the employer to be free to join or not join any union; the opposite number to union or closed shop.

Operative – A spy employed by an agency, usually having a secret designation.

Organizational picketing – Picketing of an employer in an attempt to induce the employees to join the union.

Outlawed strike—Strike forbidden by law. See *Unauthorized strike*.

Outside man—Spy under a cover but not masquerading as an employee in a plant. See *Missionary*.

Outside union—Nationally organized union seeking to organize workers in a plant previously unorganized or organized in a plant union.

Overtime — Period worked in excess of a standard workday or workweek, for which time a wage rate above the standard is usually paid; money received for overtime work.

Paper jurisdiction—Claim of a union to organizational rights over a certain class of employees when actually no attempt has been made to organize them.

Paper local—A local union issued a charter by the parent organization before any members have been enrolled in the local. Paper locals figured in a joint board election investigated by the McClellan Committee, the votes of the paper locals having been used to swing the election.

Picketing—Advertising, usually by members of a union carrying signs, the existence of a labor dispute and the union's version of its merits.

Piecework—Work done for wages based on output rather than on time spent.

Plant union — Organization of employees confined to one plant or factory.

Plant unit—Bargaining unit consisting of all production and maintenance workers in a plant regardless of type of work performed.

Political expenditures—Money spent by unions or corporations in con-

nection with the nomination or election of federal officials. Such expenditures are forbidden by the Federal Corrupt Practices Act unless, in the case of unions, they are made from "voluntary" contributions of union members.

Preferential shop—Arrangement with a union under which employer agrees to give certain preferences to union members in the matter of hiring or to require that a certain proportion of employees be members of the union.

Professional employee — Employees qualifying as "professional" under Sec. 2 (12) of the Taft-Hartley Act. They may not be included in a unit containing nonprofessional employees unless they so elect.

Publicity picketing—Another term for picketing aimed at publicizing a labor dispute. See *Informational picketing*.

Racketeer—Union official who uses his position to extort money from employers, usually by threatening to cause a strike.

Railway Labor Act—A federal law establishing administrative bodies and procedures for the prompt and orderly settlement of labor disputes between interstate carriers by rail and air and their employees and guaranteeing self-organization and collective bargaining rights to such carriers and employees.

Rank and File—Members of a union other than the officers.

Rat—Slightly stronger form of "scab." See *Scab*.

Recognition—Treating with a union as bargaining agent for employees, either for all or for those only who are members of the union.

Recognition picketing—Picketing for the object of inducing or compelling the employer to recognize the union as bargaining agent for the employer's employees. Recognition picketing conducted under certain circumstances was made an unfair labor practice by the 1959 amendments to the Taft-Hartley Act.

Referendum—Special election under some state laws in which employees are polled on question whether they wish to authorize their bargaining agent to sign a union-security contract or to rescind such authority previously granted.

Regional Director — Official of the National Labor Relations Board who acts for the Board in a specified region.

Reinstatement—Return to employment of persons unlawfully discharged.

Remedial order—See *Affirmative order.*

Representation election — See *Employee election.*

Restraint and coercion—Term used in Section 8(b) (1) of Taft-Hartley Act making it an unfair labor practice for a union to restrain or coerce employees in the exercise of their rights to join unions or to engage in union activities or in the exercise of their rights to refrain from joining unions or engaging in such activities.

Right to work—A term used to describe laws which ban union-security agreements by forbidding contracts making employment conditional on membership or nonmembership in labor organizations.

Roping—Securing information by striking up acquaintance or friendship with union men.

Run-away shop—Plant moved by employer to avoid bargaining with a union representing his employees.

Run-off election — Second employee election directed by a labor board when the first fails to show more than half the votes recorded for any one choice presented.

Sabotage—Malicious damage done by employee to employer's equipment or other property.

Scab—Epithet applied to nonstriking employee by fellow employees on strike, carrying significance of "traitor."

Secondary boycott—Refusal to deal with or buy goods from a concern which is the customer or supplier of an employer with whom the boycotters have a dispute. An indirect pressure is thus brought upon the primary object of the boycott.

Secondary strike—A strike against an employer to force him to use pressure upon another employer, usually a supplier or customer, to induce the other employer to accede to demands of the union upon him.

Self-organization—Self-determined activity by employees in the formation of labor unions.

Seniority — Length of service with an employer or in one branch of a business; preference accorded employees on the basis of length of service.

Settlement agreement—Terms agreed upon in the settlement of charges before the NLRB without a full-dress hearing, decision, and order. To be binding, such agreements must have the consent of the NLRB.

Shadowing—Operation of keeping a person under secret surveillance.

Share-the-work plan — Arrangement under which, in lieu of cutting payroll when work falls off, the hours worked by each employee are shortened.

Shop steward—Person designated by a union to take up with the foreman or supervisor the grievances of fellow employees as they arise.

Shop unit—Subdivision of a union consisting of members employed in a single shop. Its affairs are ordinarily subject to decisions by a local. See *Local.*

Showing of interest—Support union must show among employees in bargaining unit before NLRB will process union's election petition. The Board requires a union that is seeking a representation election to make a showing of interest among 30 percent of the employees in the bargaining unit.

Shutdown—Temporary closing of plant, usually because of slack work or for changing plant equipment.

Sit-down strike—Stoppage of work where the strikers remain in occupancy of the employer's premises.

Slowdown—Concerted slackening of pace in working as a means of enforcing demands made by employees.

Slugger—Specialized type of fink used to attack, assault, and beat up strikers and union leaders. Generally armed. See *Fink.*

Soldiering—Deliberate slackening of pace in work, usually as a protest against uncorrected grievances.

Speed-up—Quickening the pace of operations performed by employees, usually through stepping up the speed of machines which they attend.

Statute of limitations—As applied to unfair labor practices, a provision of the Taft-Hartley Act under which charges are outlawed if based on events more than six months old.

Stool pigeon—Person acting as industrial spy and agent provocateur.

Stranger picketing — Picketing conducted by persons who are not employees of the picketed employer. It has been held unlawful under the laws of some states.

Stretch-out—Increasing work quota of employees, usually by increasing number of operations to be performed or of machines to be watched.

Strike—Concerted cessation of work as a form of economic pressure by employees, usually organized, to enforce acceptance of their terms.

Strikebreaker — One whose trade it is to take employment in struck plants. Distinguishable from "scab," who is a workman. May pretend to work in the plant or act as a guard.

Strike vote—Balloting or canvass on question of calling a strike.

Struck work—Work performed by employees of one employer that would have been performed by employees of another employer had they not been on strike.

Subcontracting—Farming out of part of a plant's work to another company. Such diversion of work for the purpose of avoiding or evading the duty to bargain with a union is an unfair labor practice under the Taft-Hartley Act.

Superseniority—Seniority granted by contract to certain classes of employees in excess of that which length of service would justify and which is protected against reduction by events which would have the effect of reducing seniority of other employees. Union stewards and veterans are sometimes accorded superseniority. The granting of superseniority to strikers' replacements has been held to be an unfair labor practice.

Supervisor—An employee with authority to hire and fire or make effective recommendations to this effect. Supervisors enjoy no protection of bargaining rights under the Taft-Hartley Act.

Supplemental unemployment benefits—Employer-financed payments to laid-off employees to supplement the state unemployment benefits they receive.

Surveillance—Keeping watch on employees to detect evidence of union activity.

Sympathetic strike—Strike called for the purpose of influencing outcome of a dispute in another enterprise or industry.

Taft-Hartley Act—Popular name of Labor Management Relations Act, 1947, which became law June 23, 1947. Title I consists of the National Labor Relations Act as amended in 1947.

Unauthorized strike—A strike by employees contrary to the advice or without the consent of their union.

Unfair employment practice—Discrimination in employment based on race, color, religion, sex, or national origin. Forbidden by federal and some state laws.

Unfair labor practice—Practice forbidden by the National and several State Labor Relations Acts.

Unfair labor practice strike—Strike caused or prolonged in whole or in part by the employer's unfair labor practices. In such a strike, the employer must reinstate the strikers in their jobs, upon unconditional application, even though it is necessary to let replacements go.

Unfair list—Names of employers publicized by unions as "unfair" because of their refusal to recognize the union or because of some other dispute.

Union—Labor organization.

Union hiring—System under which new employees must be chosen from among union members, the union determining the members to be taken on.

Union insignia—Buttons or other signs worn by employees to indicate that they are union members. Prohibition against their display has been held unlawful interference with organizational rights, absent unusual circumstances.

Union label—Marks placed on goods indicating that they have been made in a shop which deals with a labor union.

Union shop—Arrangement with a union by which employer may hire any employee, union or non-union, but the new employee must join the union within a specified time and remain a member in good standing.

Unit—Shortened form of "unit appropriate for collective bargaining." It consists of all employees entitled to select a single agent to represent them in bargaining collectively.

Wagner Act—National Labor Relations Act, approved July 5, 1935. So called from its chief sponsor, Senator Robert F. Wagner, of New York.

Walkout—Strike in which workers leave the shop or plant.

Welfare and Pension Plans Disclosure Act—Federal law enacted in 1958 and amended in 1962 establishing reporting, disclosure, and regulatory requirements for employee welfare and pension plans.

Welfare plan—Arrangements with a union under which insurance and other benefits will be paid to employees and their families. Employer contributions are forbidden except under conditions laid down in Sec. 302 of the Taft-Hartley Act.

Wildcat strike—Unauthorized strike. See *Outlawed strike.*

Work jurisdiction—Right claimed by union under its charter to have its members and no others engaged in certain work. See *Jurisdictional dispute, Jurisdictional strike.*

Work permit—Card issued by union having closed shop to show permission that holder, though not a full-fledged union member, may be employed under contract.

Yellow-dog contract—Agreement under which an employee undertakes not to join a union while working for his employer.

Zipper clause—Clause that seeks to close all employment terms for the duration of the labor contract by stating that the agreement is "complete in itself" and "sets forth all terms and conditions" of the agreement.

INDEX

(See also Glossary of Labor Terms, p. 123)

139